SPIRITUAL
INTELLIGENCE

"Kris Vallotton's latest breakthrough work introduces the reader to the concept that one's spiritual intelligence quotient is determined by the level to which that person understands that the Holy Spirit is speaking continually. Kris implores the reader to learn to think like God by pressing into the mind of Christ. As you read this book, these new concepts will shift, adjust and change your heart and raise your spiritual game!"

Bob Hasson, author, The Business of Honor (with Danny Silk);
business consultant; CEO, RM Hasson, Inc.

"With profound insights into the marriage between neuroscience and the invitation to think with the Holy Spirit, Kris Vallotton opens a new reality of spiritual intelligence that moves past our natural-realm thinking into divine thinking from heaven's perspective. He places us in position to become agents of change and cultural transformation. Kris's hilarious stories, supernatural exploits and clear, practical guidance will make you hungry to begin your own unique journey into the realm of spiritual intelligence."

Lauren Hasson, founder and director, Lifestreams Ministries

"I've had the privilege of watching the message of this book form in Kris's heart and mind until it brought about God's intended impact on his life. And now it's positioned to change the reader. This book imparts the thrill of divine wisdom as it empowers us with purpose and a sense of destiny while we engage in this unearned partnership with God. It is far beyond our wildest dreams. It is time to stand in our call to manifest the hope-filled mind of Christ to the earth."

Bill Johnson, senior leader, Bethel Church; author, The Way of Life,
Raising Giant-Killers, The Mind of God and more

"Kris makes me think. And so does this book! He provides helpful perspective, challenging revelation and fresh insight. I have a whole new mindset around being transformed by the renewing of your mind. You'll be a better leader and more able to cultivate a Kingdom worldview in those you lead."

Brad Lomenick, author, The Catalyst Leader and H3 Leadership;
former president, Catalyst

"Spiritual Intelligence leads the reader to experience the mind of Christ—which is supernatural—instead of depending on mere human intelligence alone to figure out how to live victoriously and deal with life's many challenges. Kris uses solid biblical and prophetic insight to teach us, in a very practical way, how to discern spiritual realities and discover our true intelligence—which is spiritual plus natural. I strongly recommend this book and am proud of Kris for releasing yet another powerful resource to edify the Church and reach the world for Jesus."

Apostle Guillermo Maldonado, King Jesus International Ministry

"*Spiritual Intelligence* is more than a book. It is a prophetic call to an apostolic mission. The invitation of the Holy Spirit is upon us to release a fresh expression of being the light of the world and a city set on a hill. For too long, the prophetic gifts and graces have been used only for pointing out what is wrong. It's time for the Church, as a spiritual intelligence community, to be part of the solution. *Spiritual Intelligence* transforms us from having power to living powerfully. Jesus is the way, the truth and the life, and this book reveals the way to access truth that solves real-life challenges and glorifies the name of our Lord Jesus."

Dan McCollam, founder, Prophetic Company;
creator, ACTIVATE prophecy training model;
author, *Bending Time* and more

"In this incredibly hopeful and accessible book, Pastor Kris Vallotton draws insights from the Bible and gives practical examples that are challenging and even awe-inspiring. If you are yearning to go from knowing *about* God to hearing His voice (and recognizing the counterfeits), *Spiritual Intelligence* is the book for you."

Eric Metaxas, #1 *New York Times* bestselling author;
host, *Eric Metaxas Radio Show*

"Okay, here is something to be excited about! Kris Vallotton is about to open up a whole new context for measuring our intelligent interactions, intuitions and responses to what heaven is doing on the earth. Kris shows that our five senses act like sensory gathering mechanisms, but in our spiritual capacity. We can feel, think, see, know and hear in such a way that allows us to access God's leading into supernatural ways of life. I highly recommend that you read *Spiritual Intelligence* and allow God to strengthen you, body, soul and spirit."

Danny Silk, president, Loving on Purpose;
author, *Keep Your Love On* and more

SPIRITUAL INTELLIGENCE

THE ART *of* THINKING LIKE GOD

KRIS VALLOTTON

Chosen

a division of Baker Publishing Group
Minneapolis, Minnesota

Published by Chosen Books
11400 Hampshire Avenue South
Bloomington, Minnesota 55438
www.chosenbooks.com

Chosen Books is a division of
Baker Publishing Group, Grand Rapids, Michigan

Printed in the United States of America

Library of Congress Control Number: 2020943561

ISBN 978-0-8007-6180-6 (cloth)
ISBN 978-0-8007-6181-3 (paperback)

Unless otherwise indicated, Scripture quotations are from the New American Standard Bible® (NASB), copyright © 1960, 1962, 1963, 1968, 1971, 1972, 1973, 1975, 1977, 1995 by The Lockman Foundation. Used by permission. www.Lockman.org

Scripture quotations identified AMPC are from the Amplified® Bible (AMPC), copyright © 1954, 1958, 1962, 1964, 1965, 1987 by The Lockman Foundation. Used by permission. www.Lockman.org

Scripture quotations identified NIV are from THE HOLY BIBLE, NEW INTERNATIONAL VERSION®, NIV® Copyright © 1973, 1978, 1984, 2011 by Biblica, Inc.® Used by permission. All rights reserved worldwide.

Scripture quotations identified NKJV are from the New King James Version®. Copyright © 1982 by Thomas Nelson. Used by permission. All rights reserved.

Cover design by LOOK Design Studio

21 22 23 24 25 26   7 6 5 4 3 2

green press INITIATIVE

I dedicate this book to all the His-story makers disguised as ordinary humans living normal lives, but who are actually sons and daughters of God who have the mind of Christ. You are the Lord's secret service, His ambassadors of heaven who walk in power, think like God and love the *hell* out of people. May He hide you everywhere, from the palaces of royalty to the streets of obscurity, and may you transform everything your heart has the opportunity to touch.

Contents

Foreword

As a neuroscientist and clinician, I believe that God delights in partnering with humanity in bringing scientific breakthrough through divine insight. That's why Kris Vallotton's new book, *Spiritual Intelligence*, is a revolutionary work as he interweaves principles of science with biblical foundations. Throughout this book, Kris bridges the divide between Spirit and science—a chasm that was not created by our Creator.

Filled with practical strategies for partnering with the Holy Spirit, *Spiritual Intelligence* has the power to propel readers deep into the mind of Christ, expanding their spiritual capacity for brilliance. This book is a written record of why living with a renewed mind is not simply good theology; rather, it's one way God profoundly brings transformative health to our entire being (mind, body and spirit).

This book is for the visionaries and the pioneers, the scientists and the innovators, the mothers and the fathers, and the future generations who will have learned the art of thinking like God so that they might deliver supernatural solutions with His divine wisdom. To those of you who dare, prepare to be inspired!

Karen Garnaas, M.D., neurologist, Catalyst Neuromedical
Center PC, Redding, California

Acknowledgments

There are so many people who have poured into my life and helped me grow, but my grandfather (whose nickname was "Sparky") was the only man ever to believe in me in my growing-up years. His intense love for me shaped my life, his hard work ethic molded my character, and his patience helped form my nature. I had the privilege of leading him to the Lord the year before he went home to heaven. He was a devout atheist most of his life, yet he had a radical conversion—including several powerful spiritual experiences and multiple angelic visitations! In light of the incredible revelation he received from the Lord in those few months before he passed, and in light of the amazing, ongoing impact it had on my personal life, I wanted to acknowledge him as the pioneer of spiritual intelligence in our family.

1

Thinking Tri-Dimensionally

What does it mean to think like God, to have the mind of Christ? Sometimes we get lost in the theology of a profound truth and never really experience the reality of it. My journey into the mind of Christ began many years ago, when Bill Johnson became the senior pastor of our small Assembly of God church in Weaverville, California. In the first couple of years of his pastorate, Bill taught our congregation about the gifts of the Holy Spirit. He would teach from the Scriptures in the Sunday morning services, and Sunday evenings we would practice what we had learned by experimenting with the Holy Spirit on each other. Little did I know then that I was about to increase my spiritual horizon dramatically.

Let me explain. At that time, Kathy and I owned an automotive repair shop. One of our largest fleet customers was a timber company. They had about twenty trucks we took care of for them. This particular year, they had purchased several brand-new, identical Chevy pickups. Sadly, within a month, the first one died and came in behind a tow truck. These were the early years of computer-controlled vehicles, so there was not a lot of information about the technology available yet. I worked on that dang truck for three days, but I could not get it started. I finally called this fleet customer back and asked to have the thing towed to the Chevy dealer in Redding, about 45 miles away. The manager said, "We have ten more brand-new trucks just like this one, so figure it out."

After that conversation, I spent several more hours working on that truck. In fact, I even called the Chevy dealer. Their technician faxed me the wiring diagram and walked me through numerous tests over the phone, but nothing worked!

Finally, Sunday came around. That week, we were learning about *words of knowledge* in church. A word of knowledge is specific information we get from the Holy Spirit that is currently true about a person, place or thing, but that we could not have known, had the Lord not revealed it to us. All the words of knowledge we experienced in church were about people. During that evening's practical exercise, I began wondering if the Spirit knew anything about trucks. When Monday rolled around, I decided I would again work on the Beast—the name I had given to that uncircumcised Chevy truck that was kicking my butt.

I ate dinner and went back to work after the shop closed, praying for God's help. I suddenly had an idea that was kind of freaky. In my mind's eye, I envisioned myself laying hands on the truck in the same way that I did with people. *Okay*, I thought, *what do I have to lose? No one will see me.* So I put my hands on the fender of the Beast and prayed a sort of "help me, Jesus" prayer. Suddenly, a picture emerged in my imagination of a broken wire under the right front fender well. Then I heard a Voice in my mind say, *There is a wire broken on a diode under the right front fender.*

The problem was, I had worked on this thing for four days and there was nothing in the manual about a diode under the fender well, or anywhere else for that matter. *What the heck*, I thought, *what do I have to lose?* So I put the Beast on the rack and took it up in the air. I got my trusty flashlight out and searched the fender well like a miner looking for gold. The well was covered in undercoating, so it was hard to see, but sure enough there was a wire broken off a component. I carefully soldered the wire back on, and the Beast came to life!

This experience opened the door to a whole new dynamic in my life. From that point on, I began to grow progressively in my connection to the Holy Spirit's transcendent thinking. Over the next couple of decades, I solved numerous difficult situations in our business and life with information the Holy Spirit provided.

Google Smart

Now, let's fast-forward about forty years, to March 2018. A team from Bethel School of Technology gathered with about two hundred Google employees at Google headquarters in Silicon Valley for a *Talks at Google* session with the topic of "Furthering the Narrative around Christianity's Impact in the Tech Space." Google webcast the session live on the company's closed network so all their employees had access to it. (Many of these Google talks are also published on YouTube for everyone, although not this particular session.)

Some of the brightest minds in the world were in attendance, including several Google team members who worked in the artificial intelligence (AI) division. The talk also incorporated a Q&A panel where our team addressed live questions posed by the attendees. The results were stunning! The attendees all understood IQ, EQ and even AI, but none of them had ever even heard of SQ (meaning spiritual intelligence quotient).

I led the teaching portion of the session with this introduction: "The brightest minds in the world today are still essentially relegated to IQ and EQ, virtually ignoring the deeper dimensions of our spiritual capacity for brilliance."

I went on to explain to the Google employees how this dynamic has relegated higher education to training only our finite intellect, while disregarding the infinite nature of our redeemed spirit-man.

Journey into the New World of SQ

The silver lining of this spiritual *inexperience* presents believers with a fantastic opportunity to explore the nature of this whole new world. Like the famous astronaut Neil Armstrong, the first man ever to step foot on the moon, or like Jacques Cousteau, the great undersea explorer who searched the depths of the ocean, we are embarking on a journey to uncover the mysteries of the Divine Mind. Yet unlike Armstrong, we are not the first explorers to step foot on this firmament. Numerous ancient pioneers have forged this path, braved ridicule and uncovered many of the mysteries of God's Celestial Intellect.

One of the most famous ancient explorers in this regard was the great first-century apostle Paul. Although he was not the first human ever to experience the ability to think transcendently, he was one of the first ever to articulate his experience with a level of understanding that inspired many other explorers to join the journey.

The apostle Paul inspired this expedition when he exhorted us as believers to "be renewed in the *spirit of your mind*" (Ephesians 4:23 NKJV, emphasis added). On the surface, this seems like a simple exhortation to learn to think well, but upon deeper examination, the ramifications of Paul's insight are stunning. Notice that Paul instructs us to renew not the lower dimensions of thinking, represented in modern times by IQ and/or EQ, but the "spirit of your mind."

I realize the terms *intelligence quotient* and *emotional quotient* were not used in Paul's day, yet despite the terms, the great apostle was intimately familiar with higher education. At the age of thirteen, young Saul was sent to Palestine to learn from a rabbi named Gamaliel. (Saul's name was later changed to Paul.) Under Gamaliel, Saul mastered Jewish history, the psalms and the works of the prophets. His education would continue for the next five or six years, as he learned such things as dissecting Scripture. Saul then went on to become a lawyer and was no doubt looking to becoming a member of the Sanhedrin, the Jewish Supreme Court of 71 men who ruled over Jewish life and religion. Thus, Paul's exhortation to be renewed in the "spirit" of our minds was not a slip of the tongue or a figure of speech. No! He was intentionally instructing us to give attention to a *specific* dimension of thinking.

Mind—Your Business

Let's take a deeper look into the insights of this first-century explorer. Writing to a Greek church in the city of Corinth, Paul seeks to contrast the difference between the natural dimensions of wisdom and the divine wisdom available exclusively to believers. He explains it this way:

> When I came to you, brethren, I did not come with superiority of speech or of wisdom, proclaiming to you the testimony of God. For I determined to know nothing among you except Jesus Christ, and Him crucified. I was with you in weakness and in fear and in much trembling, and my message and my preaching were not in persuasive words of wisdom, but in demonstration of the Spirit and of power, so that your faith would not rest on the wisdom of men, but on the power of God.
>
> 1 Corinthians 2:1–5

Paul makes it clear to this Greek congregation that he is proactively restricting himself from accessing the wisdom of man so that he can demonstrate the superior benefits of God's divine power and wisdom. Paul goes on to teach them how to access the mind of Christ so that they can think like God. He writes:

> Yet we do speak wisdom among those who are mature; a wisdom, however, not of this age nor of the rulers of this age, who are passing away; but we speak God's wisdom in a mystery, the hidden wisdom which God predestined before the ages to our glory; the wisdom

which none of the rulers of this age has understood; for if they had understood it they would not have crucified the Lord of glory; but just as it is written,

> "Things which eye has not seen and ear has not heard,
> And which have not entered the heart of man,
> All that God has prepared for those who love Him."

For to us God revealed them through the Spirit; for the Spirit searches all things, even the depths of God. For who among men knows the thoughts of a man except the spirit of the man which is in him? Even so the thoughts of God no one knows except the Spirit of God. Now we have received, not the spirit of the world, but the Spirit who is from God, so that we may know the things freely given to us by God, which things we also speak, not in words taught by human wisdom, but in those taught by the Spirit, combining spiritual thoughts with spiritual words.

But a natural man does not accept the things of the Spirit of God, for they are foolishness to him; and he cannot understand them, because they are spiritually appraised. But he who is spiritual appraises all things, yet he himself is appraised by no one. *For who has known the mind of the Lord, that he will instruct Him?* But we have the mind of Christ.

1 Corinthians 2:6–16

Paul begins his insights with the fact that we have access to a dimension of wisdom that is otherworldly and inaccessible to those who don't know God. He makes three observations about this divine wisdom:

1. *It's a mystery*, which is the Greek word *musterion*,* meaning "secret doctrine." In fact, Paul goes on to tell the Corinthians, "Let a man regard us in this manner, as servants of

---

* The definitions I provide of Greek and Hebrew words throughout are all taken from *Strong's Concordance*, which is readily available at various Bible study sites online.

Christ and *stewards* of the *mysteries* of God" (1 Corinthians 4:1, emphasis added). We are actually stewards of the intellectual properties of God!

2. *It's hidden from unbelievers, but available for believers.* Solomon put it this way: "It is the glory of God to conceal a matter, but the glory of kings is to search out a matter" (Proverbs 25:2).

3. *It displays our glory.* In the days of King Solomon, God's infinite wisdom was put on display for the queen of Sheba, leaving her stunned and breathless. Likewise, the wisdom of God's Holy Spirit is to be demonstrated through His people to the world around us. This divine demonstration not only brings glory to God; it also glorifies His people. It is probably important to mention here that Jesus prayed, "The glory which You have given Me I have given to them, that they may be one, just as We are one" (John 17:22). God shares His glory with His sons and daughters.

To understand Paul's extraordinary teaching, it is important to note that the *italicized* verses in the 1 Corinthians 2 passage are quotes from the Old Testament prophet Isaiah. They provide a beautiful contrast between believers who lived before the cross and believers who live through the power of the cross, who are "born again" and live as "new creations." This divine disparity is also evident in those who today have not yet accepted Christ and therefore have not experienced the transforming power of the cross in their lives. This relegates them to drawing only from the wisdom of man and excludes them from the mind of Christ. (By the way, if you are reading this book and you don't know Jesus, this is a great time just to *stop* and ask Him into your life!)

In the passage, the prophet Isaiah makes a strong statement about the fact that no one knows the will of God. He proclaims that *eye has not seen and ear has not heard* the things God wants to do for

His people. Yet Paul answers the prophet of old by making it clear that those things they did not know back then, we know now because we have *God's* Spirit within us. His Spirit gives us access to His mind and thoughts. Isaiah the prophet goes on to ask a profound question: *Who has known the mind of the* Lord, *that he will instruct Him?*

Paul answers in effect, "We know! We have the mind of Christ."

"How do we actually have access to God's mind?" you ask. Paul says that the Holy Spirit knows the thoughts of God, and that the Holy Spirit lives in us. Consequently, we have access to God's Spirit, and having that access essentially gives us the ability to think like God! You heard me right: If you are a follower of Jesus, you can and should think like God. This is true spiritual intelligence.

Divine Smartphone

Let me clarify with a modern-day parable how spiritual intelligence works. Our smartphone is a great illustration of the way IQ, EQ and even SQ all work. Like a smartphone that has a finite amount of information stored in its memory, IQ and EQ are limited to the storage capacity of our human brains. We can increase our smartphone's memory, yet ultimately, its capacity is still relatively limited by the size of the phone. Likewise, we can increase what is stored in our own memory through education, experience, etc., but our brain's storage capacity is still finite.

On the other hand, when our smartphone connects to cellular data or Wi-Fi, suddenly we have the ability to access the Internet, which has billions of times more information than could ever be stored on a smartphone's memory. In the same way, when we connect to the Holy Spirit, we access the mind of Christ, and we tap into the Infinite One who knows *everything*! In fact, spiritual intelligence transcends IQ and EQ in the same way that the Internet has a billion times more information than the memory on our smartphone. Again, SQ is not just accessing your own spirit or brain. Instead, it is connecting with God's Spirit, who is eternal, has all knowledge and wisdom, and knows the future.

Furthermore, the Holy Spirit has unfathomable experience with humankind and knows the heart of every person on the planet. The Spirit is the Genius of geniuses, the Scientist of scientists, the Doctor of doctors, the Engineer of engineers . . . you get the idea. He is the real definition of true brilliance. Think about it like this: The mind of Christ gives us access to the Internet of divine wisdom, which is the ultimate spiritual intelligence. Intrigued? Stay tuned, because the best is yet to come!

2

Renewing Your Mind

The apostle Paul, who was the great first-century spiritual explorer, wrote, "Do not be conformed to this world, but be transformed by the renewing of your mind" (Romans 12:2). The critical question here is *how* do we renew our minds so that we live in our divine advantage? How do we practically move from concept to prototype, and from prototype to production, so to speak, so that we can live a lifestyle of transcended thinking? Before we get too deep into the concept of transcended thinking, however, let's explore the natural mind and the intriguing subject of neuroscience.

I found myself thrust into the topic of neuroscience in 2008, when I had a mental and emotional breakdown that lasted nearly a year. I lay on the couch for six months, completely incapacitated, overwhelmed with anxiety and drowning in the throes of depression. I had experienced anxiety throughout much of my life, but I had never known a day of depression. I sought help through several professional counselors, and although it was good to talk to people who cared, none of them really helped me much. It was not that they didn't try; it was more that they didn't have the expertise I needed for my situation.

In my desperation to get well, I started reading a few books on neuroscience, in particular a book called *Who Switched Off My Brain?* by Dr. Caroline Leaf (Thomas Nelson, 2009), who is herself a neuroscientist and a strong believer. I learned from Dr. Leaf that our thoughts travel on brain highways called neural pathways. (You can picture neural pathways like the result when a hot marble is dropped through a block of cheese.) Metaphorically speaking, the wider the highway, the easier it is to repeat the same thought. And the more we repeat the same thought, the wider the physical highways in our brains get. You can see from my simple explanation how easy it is to create a brain hamster wheel—a superhighway of constructive or destructive mindsets.

Another interesting fact about our brains' mode of operation comes from Donald Miller, an American author, speaker and the CEO of StoryBrand. According to Miller's research, when our brains draw a conclusion about something, they use the least amount of energy to get to that conclusion. He gave a great illustration of the way our brains process information when he spoke at our Bethel Leaders Conference at the Civic Auditorium in Redding, California, about five miles from our Bethel Church campus. He asked, "How many of you took the shortest route here from the church?"

Of course, most of the attendees raised their hands.

Miller replied, "I bet you didn't! The shortest route is as the crow flies, but I'm thinking that most everyone here took the highway."

The point he was making is that our minds take the quickest route, like a crow that disregards the paths of highways and byways and flies the shortest distance and quickest route from one point to another. Just as it is challenging to convince a crow to fly the exact route of a highway, it is challenging to direct our minds to go a different route than what they are accustomed to. This is such a powerful image of *how* we think and why it can be difficult to change our minds about life.

Let me introduce one more neuroscience concept called "the principle of first mention." This principle states that the first time you hear information about any subject, it becomes the *way* in which you view that topic from that point on. In other words, the information you receive first about something creates the lens by which you view that subject. Everything you hear or experience after the first exposure to that topic will be processed through the information you received first. The "first mention" info creates a *truth lens* by which you measure and/or evaluate all other proceeding info concerning that theme. This of course creates a number of concerns, the primary concern being the unhealthy dynamic that takes place when "first mention" information is wrong or inaccurate.

For instance, let's suppose that you are the parent of a twelve-year-old son, and one of his friends exposes him to pornography before you teach him about healthy sexuality. A year later, you sit down to have "the Talk" with your son, and unfortunately, he is forced to process your words through a porn filter—not because it is right, but because it was mentioned to him first. Can he make a conscious choice to reject his "first mention" core value system and embrace the truth? Yes! But he will *proactively* have to forsake the lies he was taught and renew his mind with the truth. This will not happen by accident.

The Lord created us to process information in this first mention way so that we—especially as parents, but also as mentors and leaders—can cultivate a Kingdom worldview in the life of those we raise or lead *first*. When our children or disciples hear the truth from us first, then they are prepared to face the world full of deception and process what they hear through the truth lens already in place inside them.

Bulldozing New Neural Pathways

Now that we have had a crash course in neuroscience, let's look at Paul's exhortation for us to renew our minds and ultimately to embrace spiritual intelligence. Remember that he wrote, "Do not be conformed to this world, but be transformed by the renewing of your mind" (Romans 12:2). Much of what is being taught about the renewed mind today is behavior modification and not transformation. So how do we renew our mind, and how do we know when we have a renewed mind? Here are eight symptoms of having a transformed mind:

1. You are full of hope.
2. The impossible seems reasonable.
3. You live in peace and you don't worry; your speculations are positive.
4. You like yourself and even rejoice in your weakness, knowing that when and where you are weak, God is strong.
5. You are quick to forgive, and you freely give others grace and mercy.
6. You are confident and thankful.
7. You believe in others and give them the benefit of the doubt.
8. You know how to think tri-dimensionally.

Obviously, this is not a complete list of the broad spectrum of the renewed mind. It is more like the cheat sheet you get when you buy a new car and the manufacturer knows you aren't going to read the three-hundred-page manual before you take it for a spin. Hence, you are given three pages of colorful card stock and an info bulletin that usually hangs from the mirror and says in huge letters *READ THIS before operating this vehicle!*

Let's say you are looking at the renewed mind cheat sheet of eight symptoms and you think, *No, no, no, no, no, no, no and no! Now what do I do?*

The first thing you do is begin to meditate! I know that when you hear the word *meditate*, you probably picture some guy sitting on the floor with his legs crossed, humming to himself, trying to empty his brain of all thoughts. But thankfully, this is not scriptural meditation. Meditation that focuses on emptying your brain is not going to lead to a renewed mind.

Let me introduce you to the guy in the Bible who exposed me to real meditation that actually transformed my mind. His name is Joshua, and his story is pretty compelling. The guy followed a leader who talked to God face-to-face. Moses was his name. God Himself tasked Moses with rescuing the Israelites from the bondage of four hundred years of slavery in Egypt and bringing them into their Promised Land, the land of Canaan.

You likely have read the biblical account. Moses demanded that Pharaoh free God's people, and eight plagues later, with Egypt in shambles, Pharaoh finally capitulated . . . sort of. After the Israelites left the country, Pharaoh had a change of heart. I mean, the man had a classic case of a hard heart. Mustering his army, he chased God's people to the edge of the Red Sea.

Trapped between the pursuing enemy army and the Red Sea, Moses cried out to God while the Israelites moaned in terror. Suddenly God, working in partnership with Moses, parted the Red Sea, and the Israelites crossed over on dry land. Then Pharaoh's army rode across the sea floor and God released the raging waters on top of them, drowning them. The people of God were saved, and stage one of the mission was complete.

Part two of the great commission was for Moses to lead the Israelites through the wilderness, across the Jordan River and into the Promised Land. But after forty years of trying, Moses died. The most famous leader in the history of the world at the time, a man who spoke to God face-to-face, a man who parted the Red Sea and did countless miracles, left this task unfinished. It then fell to his servant Joshua. God Himself broke the news to Joshua, proclaiming, "Moses My servant is dead; now therefore arise, cross this Jordan, you and all this people, to the land which I am giving to them, to the sons of Israel" (Joshua 1:2).

I can only imagine the stress that must have fallen on Josh that day. His mentor was gone, the people were stressed out, and God was giving him an impossible mandate. Yet God shared a secret with Joshua that would ultimately be the key ingredient to his profound success. God exhorted Joshua several times to "be strong and coura-geous," and then He finished His exhortation with these final words: "This book of the law shall not depart from your mouth, but you shall meditate on it day and night, so that you may be careful to do according to all that is written in it; for then you will make your way prosperous, and then you will have success" (Joshua 1:8).

Notice that God told Joshua in effect, "By meditating on My Word, you will make your way prosperous and have success!" I'm not sure if you caught the "you will" part. God didn't say, "*I will* make you prosperous and successful." He said, "*You* will make your way prosperous, and *you* will have success."

Seriously, this seems like an overly simplified formula for success. I mean, today we have people traveling the entire world, looking for the key to true greatness. We have life coaches, online courses, seminars and universities all promising to "change your life" and give you the secret to success. Many of these things are good, and certainly some of them can help you grow. But God's one-liner makes it clear and straightforward: Meditate on His Word, and then do it!

When we consider Joshua's circumstances, this advice does not seem like his most pressing need. Some advice more like "find some leaders, build a strategy, make a bunch of weapons and get good at war" would seem a little more relevant to Josh's situation. But God is right, and in the end Joshua succeeds.

A deeper look into the Hebrew word *meditate* yields a huge reve-lation into Joshua's success. The word *meditate* in this passage is the Hebrew word *hagah*, and it means "to growl and declare" (among a few other things). This Hebrew word is used in Isaiah 31:4, which reads, "For thus says the LORD to me, 'As the lion or the young lion *growls* over his prey . . .'" (emphasis added). The English word *growls* is that Hebrew word *hagah*, translated as "meditate" in the book of Joshua. The point is that meditation in God is not sitting in a corner humming to ourselves; it is proactively bulldozing new neural pathways into our brains. This is God's formula for a renewed mind!

For example, let's say your daughter is late coming home from school and you have a history of freaking out in these kinds of situations, as if you have a six-lane freeway in your brain to thoughts like *she must have been kidnapped*, or *maybe she was abducted by aliens!* Before you know it, you are in a full-blown panic attack. *Stop* and consider what God has said about your daughter's safety. You vaguely remember that Psalm 91 is a chapter about protection, so you open up your Bible, as if you are loading an assault rifle, and you begin to pace the floor and read the chapter out loud:

> He who dwells in the shelter of the Most High will abide in the shadow of the Almighty. I will say to the LORD, "My refuge and my fortress, my God, in whom I trust!" For it is He who delivers you from the snare of the trapper and from the deadly pestilence. He will cover you with His pinions, and under His wings you may seek refuge; His faithfulness is a shield and bulwark.
>
> You will not be afraid of the terror by night, or of the arrow that flies by day; of the pestilence that stalks in darkness, or of the destruction that lays waste at noon. A thousand may fall at your side and ten thousand at your right hand, but it shall not approach you. You will only look on with your eyes and see the recompense of the wicked. For you have made the LORD, my refuge, even the Most High, your dwelling place. No evil will befall you, nor will any plague come near your tent.
>
> For He will give His angels charge concerning you, to guard you in all your ways.
>
> Psalm 91:1–11

Remember that you are building new neural pathways in your brain, so metaphorically speaking, you are hacking a fresh trail through the uninhabited jungle of your mind. The Word of God is like a machete in your hand, and every verse you speak like a growling lion is hewing a pathway into a new way of thinking. The more often you abandon the six-lane freeway of destructive thinking and take the new walking trail of God-thoughts, the faster you will transform your mind. Soon, figuratively speaking, the six-lane freeway will be overgrown with vegetation, and the walking trail will become a *High-way*! The symptoms of a transformed mind will become natural, and like Joshua, you will be successful and prosperous.

Core Values Versus High Values

It is important to remember that the renewed mind doesn't just think differently; it also believes differently. This is expressed by the fact that there is a big difference between your *high values* and your *core values*. For instance, if you say, "God always takes care of me," but then you worry about His provision when your rent is due, your anxiety reveals that your high value is that God takes care of you, but your core value is that He really doesn't, or at least that He won't in this circumstance.

Let me explain it like this: High values are the truths you hold in the greatest regard, but core values are what you truly believe—the way you actually see the world. Jesus put it like this: "So take care how you listen" (Luke 8:18). *How* you listen is determined by your core values. Core values are the glasses your brain wears. In other words, it is not what you see, but *the way you see* it that affects your emotional state. Faith is the lens of your core-value glasses because it reveals what you actually believe deep down to be true. Faith is the difference, the catalyst, between your high values and your core values.

Let's look at it from a different perspective. Let's say you turn on the news and there is a school shooting. There are multiple victims, and the shooter has taken the principal hostage and is holed up on the campus, surrounded by a SWAT team. Now let's imagine that the same scene happens in a movie you are watching for entertainment. Your brain remembers both scenarios, but it has one compartment or room for fiction and another compartment or room for fact—or what your brain believes is reality. Although you viewed a terrible crisis at the movies, it was entertainment in that scenario because you did not believe it was true.

Jesus made a powerful statement that relates to this: "If you continue in My word, then you are truly disciples of Mine; and you will know the truth, and the truth will make you free" (John 8:31–32). The word *truth* in this passage is the Greek word *letheia*, and it means "reality." In other words, meditating on the Word of God will determine what things your mind assigns to the fiction room and what things it assigns to the fact room.

The power of the transformed mind is that it rightly divides between fact and fiction, according to your faith in God. So when your rent is due and a thought comes to your mind that says, *No provision is coming; you're going to be homeless,* the renewed mind assigns that thought to the fiction room because it is opposed to the Word of God. The transformed mind accesses the "reality" compartment of the renewed mind to decide what to "believe" and adjusts your soul's emotional state accordingly. Because you have meditated on the Word of God, your mind is able to go to the "reality compartment" and access the words of Jesus, who said,

> Do not worry then, saying, "What will we eat?" or "What will we drink?" or "What will we wear for clothing?" For the Gentiles eagerly seek all these things; for your heavenly Father knows that you need all these things. *But seek first His kingdom and His righteousness, and all these things will be added to you.*
>
> Matthew 6:31–33, emphasis added

If you read this passage in the middle of your rent situation and you still worry, your mind has assigned the passage to the fiction compartment. You remember it, but you don't believe it. It might even be a high value—something you want to be true or you think should be true, because it is true for others and it was true for Jesus, so you should believe it. But you actually don't!

Meditation is therefore more than memorizing Scripture. It is making a proactive decision to believe God, to put truth above facts, and to trust in His goodness in *your* life. Joshua-type meditation moves God's Word from memory to reality and changes your destiny.

One more time, "Do not be conformed to this world, but be transformed by the renewing of your mind" (Romans 12:2). You can't change your life, but if you change your mind, God will transform your life.

3

Discovering Your Superpowers

Somewhere around 598 BC, Nebuchadnezzar ransacked Judah and Jerusalem, climaxing in the deportation of ten thousand Jewish POWs to Babylon. The situation was bleak. The country lay in ruins, Solomon's magnificent Temple was destroyed, and a violent, vicious dictator was ruling the Israelites with a rod of iron. Amid the chaos, God had a secret strategy that would ultimately unravel the very core of wickedness in two powerful empires, including the overthrow of four kings. The plan called for God to send four of His superheroes into Babylon and later into Persia, with the divine mission of demonstrating the life and benefits of a superior Kingdom, and then introducing those countries' rulers to the King of kings. The outcome was stunning. Seventy short years later, two great empires fell into the hands of heaven, their kings giving homage to the God of Daniel, Shadrach, Meshach and Abednego.

The truth is, God created superheroes long before there was ever a comic magazine or a Marvel movie. Whether it was the four fireproof, lion-taming wise men of Babylon, or the lion-killing, bear-stomping, giant-slaying boy from the backside of the wilderness, God has always had His superheroes. They are men and women who are given incredible powers, then are dispatched into what may seem initially like suicide missions and impossible situations, with almost no chance of success. Yet at the end of the day, when the dust has cleared and the lights have dimmed, they exit the scene, dragging the head of Goliath by the hair and shouting the praises of God. (I know the illustration is a little Old Testament, but bear with me.)

In the case of Daniel and his three friends, they possessed divine wisdom and supernatural knowledge, and they (at least Daniel) understood the meaning of dreams and visions. In fact, Daniel could tell you your dream, give you the interpretation and tell you what to do about it. *Wow*, right? But before we cram that story into a cedar chest somewhere among the mothballs of ancient history, what if I told you that God is still empowering superheroes? What if renewing your mind is not just thinking well (as I explained in the previous chapter), but is divine thinking? What if I told you that you actually have a great advantage over the four boys from Babylon and the kid who killed Goliath? Crazy, right? *But true!*

We talked about renewing our minds and building neural pathways into new methods of thinking, which is formidable in transforming our personhood. Yet our "superpowers" are actually rooted in the "spirit of our mind," as I mentioned earlier. So how do we tap into the third dimension and experience divine thinking? Let me begin with some insights from the first encounter King Nebuchadnezzar had with God, which sent him on a wild journey to find his divine purpose.

I will set the scene for you: King Nebuchadnezzar is an arrogant egotist famous for his violent temper. He has a fetish for burning his servants alive while he watches. One night, the king has a dream that he knows is related to his divine destiny, but he can't figure out what it means. So he gathers the magicians, the conjurers, the sorcerers and the Chaldeans and demands that they tell him his dream and give him the interpretation.

Of course, they are freaked out and beg the king at least to tell them his dream so they can interpret it for him. But the king isn't going for it. He tells them that if they cannot tell him the dream first, he is going to rip their arms and legs off and then burn their houses down.

Daniel is on the king's "wise men council," and he isn't too excited about the death-by-dismemberment decree, so he gets to praying. Thankfully, the Lord gives him the dream and interpretation just in the nick of time. Here is Daniel's opening statement to King Nebuchadnezzar:

> As for the mystery about which the king has inquired, neither wise men, conjurers, magicians nor diviners are able to declare it to the king. However, there is a God in heaven who reveals mysteries, and He has made known to King Nebuchadnezzar what will take place in the latter days. This was your dream and the visions in your mind while on your bed. As for you, O king, while on your bed your thoughts turned to what would take place in the future; and He who reveals mysteries has made known to you what will take place.
>
> Daniel 2:27–29

What is interesting is that King Nebuchadnezzar stumbled into SQ—spiritual intelligence—when he began to inquire about the mysteries of the age to come. His inquiry transcended IQ and EQ since nobody knows the future except God, who lives from eternity. The king therefore could not answer his own questions about the future no matter how long he thought about it, because the future is unknowable without God. In case you are unfamiliar with the rest of the story, Daniel went on to tell the king his dream and give him the interpretation. Consequently, all the wise in Babylon were saved.

Forging Ahead

Now let me set this in context with the previous chapter, where we discussed how the renewing of our minds through divine meditation forges new neural pathways in our brains. Meditation is a highly effective way to renew the IQ and EQ portion of your brain, as I also discussed earlier. Yet something profound happens when we refuse to solve problems with our natural minds, and instead inquire of the Holy Spirit for His divine wisdom. This exercise begins the process of "renewing the *spirit* of our minds."

Let me put it like this: The reason we don't tap into the wisdom of the *age to come* is because we settle for the wisdom of the *age we live in*. So all our brain "freeways" are being forged to embody natural conclusions. But to tap into spiritual intelligence, we will have to exit the freeway of IQ/EQ thinking, metaphorically speaking, and get on the SQ *High*-way of divine wisdom. In other words, as long as we allow ourselves to come to *good* conclusions, we will feel no need to ask the Spirit for *God*-conclusions.

I will give you an example: Let's say you are hit with a large, unexpected expense, and you don't have the money to pay for it. So you lie awake at night thinking of various solutions to solve the problem. You could refinance your house to pay off the debt, or maybe take on another job. If the situation is dire, you might consider filing for bankruptcy. You weigh the Scriptures against your situation and make a decision based on biblical core values. This might be a reasonable way to approach the situation, yet it could rob you of God's supernatural solution.

Here is the SQ approach to the same situation: Instead of doing the "reasonable thing," you press into prayer and ask God to give you His perspective on your financial crisis. In the midst of your spiritual inquiry, you have a strong, compelling thought that you are supposed to give away your gold watch to the homeless person you saw begging on the corner of your street. *How is this going to solve my financial situation?* you wonder.

Yet the thought intensifies, and you feel gripped with the deep conviction that you *must* obey. So you get your gold watch and give it to the homeless guy down the street. Three days later, you receive a certified letter in the mail informing you that your uncle, who died twenty years ago, left you a $100,000 inheritance that you never received.

Crazy, you say? Well, think of all the ways that God provided for people in the Bible. Did you ever notice that most of the supernatural provisions in the Bible occurred in response to people's pure desperation, and not out of their divine lifestyle? Here is one of my favorite miracle stories that illustrates my point:

> Now a certain woman of the wives of the sons of the prophets cried out to Elisha, "Your servant my husband is dead, and you know that your servant feared the LORD; and the creditor has come to take my two children to be his slaves." Elisha said to her, "What shall I do for you? Tell me, what do you have in the house?" And she said, "Your maidservant has nothing in the house except a jar of oil." Then he said, "Go, borrow vessels at large for yourself from all your neighbors, even empty vessels; do not get a few. And you shall go in and shut the door behind you and your sons, and pour out into all these vessels, and you shall set aside what is full." So she went from him and shut the door behind her and her sons; they were bringing the vessels to her and she poured. When the vessels were full, she said to her son, "Bring me another vessel." And he said to her, "There is not one vessel more." And the oil stopped. Then she came and told the man of God. And he said, "Go, sell the oil and pay your debt, and you and your sons can live on the rest."
>
> 2 Kings 4:1–7

The first thing we observe in this story is that God's provision in this situation defied logic and reason. Furthermore, this widowed woman would never have received a supernatural solution if she'd had natural provision. What I am getting at is that the reason we don't develop "the spirit of our minds" is because we usually solve life's challenges with lower-level, natural thinking—thinking that can be based in biblical principles, but may not actually be Spirit led.

You might be asking yourself if I am suggesting that we not base our thinking on biblical principles. The answer is no! In the previous chapter we learned how to think biblically by meditating on God's Word, which helped make Joshua successful. Biblical thinking is life-transforming because it teaches us *how* God thinks. But the only way to know *what* God is thinking is to have a connection through the Holy Spirit to God's mind. I understand the difference here might be a little difficult to grasp at first, but it will make a profound difference in your life when you understand it. Let's revisit a few verses and dig a little deeper into their application. The apostle Paul wrote,

> For who among men knows the thoughts of a man except the spirit of the man which is in him? Even so the thoughts of God no one knows except the Spirit of God. Now we have received, not the spirit of the world, but the Spirit who is from God, so that we may know the things freely given to us by God, which things we also speak, not in words taught by human wisdom, but in those taught by the Spirit, combining spiritual thoughts with spiritual words.
>
> 1 Corinthians 2:11–13

Paul is pointing out that we have received God's Spirit, and we therefore have access to His thoughts. The apostle goes on to say that the Spirit is teaching us how to *have* God's thoughts (i.e., His imagination, visions and dreams) and His spiritual words. In this case, we are *not* just thinking *like* God; instead, we are thinking His actual thoughts planted in us by the Holy Spirit, knowing His mind in whatever situations we face, and mirroring His imagination about the solutions and outcomes in real time!

Spiritual Pathways

In order to pave new neural pathways to *divine* thinking, we will need to push past the temptation to solve the challenges of life with *biological* thinking, which is our natural inclination. Remember that Donald Miller pointed out how our brains are hardwired to draw conclusions using the least amount of energy possible. We will therefore proactively have to discipline ourselves to forgo the initial, rational conclusions in order to allow room for our divine imagination to emerge. Furthermore, we will have to get comfortable with solutions that *sometimes* defy logic and reason (although not always), to embrace God's superior thinking.

Let's look at an example from one of my favorite Old Testament stories about a guy named Gideon. The Midianites oppressed the Israelites for seven long years. The Israelites were nearly starving to death while the Midianites destroyed their fields and stole their crops. The situation grew so grim that the Israelites hid themselves in caves and concealed their food and supplies as well (see Judges 6). For instance, Gideon was threshing his wheat in a winepress to keep it from the invaders. Amid this nasty situation, Gideon had an encounter with an angel who declared, "The LORD is with you, O valiant warrior" (verse 12). Gideon seemed unimpressed and began to interrogate the angel, in effect asking, "Oh yeah? Where are all the miracles our forefathers told us about?" The interaction concludes with the angel commissioning Gideon to defeat Midian and free God's people (see verses 13–14).

Gideon then gathered 32,000 men to go out against the Midianites and Amalekites, who were "as numerous as locusts" (Judges 7:12). But God told Gideon it was too many men and that he should send home anyone who was afraid. That day 22,000 men went home, leaving 10,000 soldiers to fight. As if that weren't bad enough, then God was like, "Hey Gideon, you still have too many men; have the soldiers go down to the river and drink. The guys that lap water like a dog will be your army" (see Judges 7).

I don't know about you, but if I were Gideon, I would have been asking some questions like, "God, did the three of You talk about this? Is there anyone else up there I could speak to?" Logic and reason actually would have been looking pretty good right about then. Personally, I would have been looking for the station where I could exit that SQ train!

The dog-style lappers numbered three hundred men, but what the heck are you going to do with three hundred dog-lappers against a coalition of well-equipped soldiers from two countries? But wait, it gets worse! Gideon equips his men with three hundred torches, jars and trumpets. Did you notice anything missing from this list? Like swords, spears and bows?

Here's the real kicker: The straw that broke the camel's back for me was when God inspired Gideon to develop this crazy battle plan. Gideon proclaimed, "All right, men, here's the plan: You're going to wait until nighttime, and then you and your men are going to climb up on that hill over there. Next, I want you simultaneously to light the torches, blow the trumpets, break the jars and shout, 'For the Lord and for Gideon.'"

Really? This is Your plan, God? This is a suicide mission that makes no sense at all!

In the middle of that night, Gideon and his men commenced the crazy battle plan. The enemy soldiers became so confused that they started killing each other and fled the battlefield. Gideon's small band of dog-lapping warriors went after them, slaying them by the multitudes as they tried to escape. When the other Israelite soldiers saw Gideon's guys chasing the enemy armies, courage rose in them and they joined the fight. When the battle was over, Gideon and his band of militia had won the war and freed their people. (You can read the entire story in Judges 6–8.)

Here are five things to remember about divine thinking:

1. At first, natural thinking will often challenge our ability to build neural pathways to divine thinking, because metaphorically speaking, we have six-lane freeways already built into our lower levels of intelligence.

2. Oftentimes, God thinks outside the laws of physics since He lives in a superior reality. Many of His solutions therefore transcend the laws of nature, the facts and natural reason. It can be unnerving to wait on God, only to have Him give you a resolution that takes extreme faith and could cause you more trouble with people than the situation you are trying to resolve in the first place.

3. Renewing our minds through biblical meditation so that we think like God is life-transforming. Renewing the spirit of our minds in such a way that we are mirroring God's thoughts concerning situations, circumstances, people or things, etc., is like the *Renewed Mind 2.0.*

4. Renewing the spirit of your mind is really about learning to hear the voice of God by allowing time for your spirit to build a friendship with the Holy Spirit and ultimately bond spirit-to-Spirit.

5. Much like any other relationship, building a friendship with the Holy Spirit takes time. There is simply no substitute for experience. We begin the process by asking the Holy Spirit what He thinks about various things throughout our day, and then we listen spirit-to-Spirit for His answers.

Sovereign Protection

I have been on a lifelong journey of pursuing spiritual intelligence. In my early days with Jesus, I had just about as many failures as I had successes. But over time, it has become easier and easier to hear and understand God's interactions with me. It is always exciting to bring SQ into the realms of people who have no experience with anything beyond natural thinking. I had one of those opportunities a few years back. I was invited to minister at the Cedars—a beautiful mansion outside Washington, D.C., where leaders come from all over the world to receive ministry from Doug Coe and his team. (Doug has since passed away.) The first time I stayed at the Cedars, I had not yet met Mr. Coe, nor did he or his teams have any experience in "prophetic ministry." So my first assignment was to spend the day ministering to Doug's staff so they could test my "gift."

Early in the morning, while waiting in what was called the Lincoln Room, I looked across the way into a large ballroom and observed an elderly man having a conversation with three other people: a middle-aged man, his apparent wife, and a tall, younger man. As I watched them from the parlor, the Spirit began to talk to me about them. I asked my handler if I could give them a "word." She was not sure what a "word" was, but she thought it would probably be okay.

The handler escorted me into the ballroom and introduced me to Doug Coe, who was the elderly man I had observed. After a few minutes of introductions to the others, I asked Doug if I could share what the Spirit had told me about his three friends. "Sure," he responded with a smile.

I looked at the middle-aged man and said, "I don't know who you are, but God told me He has made you the safest man in the world! In fact, He placed you in this purple bubble, and it is impervious to every kind of weapon—bombs, bullets, biological agents . . . nothing can penetrate God's force field around you!"

His wife began to weep profusely. "Do you know who my husband is?" she inquired through her tears.

"Nope, I have no idea," I replied.

"He is the president of . . . [she named a distant country]. There have been numerous assassination attempts on his life. I haven't slept well in years," she explained.

"Well, madam, you're worrying for nothing because he's the safest man in the world!" I declared. We prayed together, they thanked me, and I went back to the Lincoln Room.

Fast-forward to a year later, when my team and I were at the D.C. National Prayer Breakfast. I was in the restroom when a man entered behind me. "Kris, do you remember me?" he inquired.

It took me a minute to recognize him, but then I recalled, "Yes, you're the safest man in the world!"

We both laughed as we hugged. "Did you hear what happened to me?" he asked.

"No, sir. What happened?"

"I went out to eat with several of my staff back home. I got a phone call on my cell phone and I couldn't hear the caller, so I stepped outside. As soon as I cleared the threshold, the entire place blew up and killed everyone inside. The debris flew around me without touching me, and a Voice said, *You are the safest man in the world!* Someone had put a bomb under my table," he explained.

What a crazy story, but it gets crazier. A couple of years later, I was back at the D.C. National Prayer Breakfast, sitting in the main room with 3,700 others. A lady at my table immediately leaned forward and asked me if I remembered her.

"No, I'm sorry; I don't recognize you," I said sheepishly.

"My husband is the safest man in the world!" she repeated with a smile.

"Oh wow, yes, of course I remember you! We met at the Cedars when I gave your husband that word."

"That's right, and have you heard what happened to him?" she asked.

"Yes, madam. He was nearly blown up a couple of years ago."

"Actually, he's been nearly blown up half a dozen times! The last time, he was on the top floor when someone blew up an entire building. He was the only one who lived. He exited the building untouched. Is there any way to take that word you gave him back?" she asked in earnest.

"Why?" I asked curiously.

"Because he doesn't think he can die, so he's going to the most dangerous places in the world and it drives me nuts," she insisted.

"I guess that's a conversation you would have to have with Jesus," I responded.

I am nobody special; we all have the same capacity for SQ. I don't share stories like this one to brag about myself. I share them to inspire you to grow and develop a deeper relationship with Jesus, so that you, too, can have your own lifelong adventure in the Spirit.

4

Duct Tape and Swords

It was the National Prayer Breakfast, where around 3,700 people gather for three days every year to hear the president of the United States address believers from every religious persuasion, and also to pray for our country. After the corporate address, people break up into smaller groups to dialogue and pray about various subjects.

I spoke to one of the groups at the prayer breakfast a few years back, at a small gathering of mostly political women (and a few men) on the subject of empowering women. After the session was over, thirty or forty people lingered in the room, talking and connecting. My wife, Kathy, and I, along with a few friends, were making small talk with a man who was a high government official in a foreign country. He told us that he would be running for president back home. His wife was with him, and they both spoke broken English. I could hardly pay attention to our conversation, however, because I was so distracted by a vision I saw of a sword sticking out of the wife's stomach. The vision was so vivid in my mind's eye that I was sure the Spirit was talking to me, but the setting made it hard to know what to do. With sweating palms and an anxious heart, I decided to take a risk. Pointing to her body, I blurted out, "You have a sword in your stomach right there!"

With a question mark on their faces, and not understanding English very well, they asked, "What? Sorry . . . no understand you?"

I repeated, this time more slowly, while making a sword gesture, "There's a sword in your stomach!"

"Sword?" she repeated.

"Yes!" I replied, nodding my head.

"Where?" she inquired.

Pointing to the exact spot on the side of her belly, I said, "There."

Her face lit up and her eyes widened. She looked over at her husband as if asking for help to find the words. Pointing to her stomach, she said, "I ha- . . . ha-ve bad pain there . . . years . . . I go to many doc- . . . doc-tor all over country."

"Yes," I interrupted, "and they couldn't find anything wrong, right?"

"*Yes! Yes!* It be true what you say!"

"But if I pull the sword out, the pain will stop," I insisted. "Can I pull the sword out?" I asked, while staring at her husband.

Meanwhile, Kathy looked as though she wanted to run out of the room screaming, so I was trying not to let our eyes meet. We stood there for what seemed like an eternity as the couple conversed in another language. Finally, they nodded their heads in agreement.

"Are you ready?" I asked, trying to lighten the serious mood. I mean, how do you ready yourself for someone to pull an invisible sword out of you?

"I don't know," she responded anxiously.

Ignoring her fear, I grabbed the handle of the sword and jerked it out of her. She suddenly became unconscious and fell backward onto the floor!

I don't know why or how, but Kathy anticipated the woman's fall and caught her head right before she hit the concrete.

Her husband started yelling, "*She fainted! She fainted!*"

I answered, "It's Jesus!"

"*Who?*" he inquired loudly, with stress all over his face.

"Jesus Christ," I countered.

"*Jesus! Jesus! Jesus!*" he shouted, obviously trying to wrap his brain around the situation.

"Yes, Jesus Christ of Nazareth," I said in a soothing voice. I'm not sure he got what I said, but at least he stopped shouting.

I looked down at his wife, who was now being prayed for by our team. Her eyes were flickering a hundred miles an hour, and I could tell she was in a spiritual trance. (If you are unfamiliar with spiritual trances, I give a detailed explanation of them in chapter 6.) Her countenance was glowing with intense peace, and she looked to be in a deep state of sleep. I had seen people in such trances many times before. The Spirit becomes their anesthesiologist, while God operates on their inner being.

I knew this lady would be all right, yet anxiety began to grow in my heart as I mentally recounted the times I had observed people being unconscious for hours at a time in this kind of situation. I started to pray under my breath for her to awaken, because I knew that soon someone would call the paramedics despite my reassurance that it was Jesus. Five intensely long minutes passed by like molasses as we waited nervously. Finally, she opened her eyes and sat up.

We all gasped in relief as she struggled to comprehend what was going on and how she had ended up on the floor. She exchanged some words we couldn't comprehend with her husband as we helped her up. Then she looked over at me and began to weep uncontrollably, her makeup streaking down her beautiful face as she motioned toward her stomach.

"All pain gone! All pain gone!" she kept repeating.

Her husband looked as if he had seen a ghost. He kept shaking his head in disbelief and saying "Wow!" (or something like it).

About an hour later, Kathy and I got into a large elevator filled with politicians as we were going back to our room. As soon as the elevator door closed, one of them said, "Hey, are you the guy that pulled that sword out of that lady?"

"Yes," I responded sheepishly, trying not to make another scene.

"Do I have any swords in me?" he asked anxiously.

His question inspired a passionate conversation with nearly everyone in the elevator. Some were recounting the story to others who had not heard it, while at the same time several people were inquiring about whether or not their own affliction had spiritual roots. The word spread quickly throughout the conference, and soon people were searching for us, wanting us to "pull swords out of them."

The Restaurant Experience

A couple of hours later, we were supposed to meet someone for lunch at the restaurant situated in the middle of the hotel, amidst a ton of foot traffic. This person brought several other women with her, so we pulled a bunch of tables together and everyone scooted in tight. The conversation quickly migrated to spiritual subjects as some of the women began to recount the sword story from their unique perspectives.

There was a beautiful younger lady sitting next to me whom I didn't know. When I made eye contact with her, I saw a piece of duct tape on her forehead with the word ABANDONED written on it. I leaned over and quietly whispered in her ear what I was seeing. Her eyes filled with tears, so I asked, "Can I rip the duct tape off your head?"

"Yes! Yes!" she begged.

I grabbed the invisible duct tape and jerked it off her head. Immediately, she fell off her chair and onto the floor in a fetal position, weeping in grief. When the woman across the table saw that, she exclaimed, "What did you do to her?!"

"Well," I said, trying to explain a spiritual deliverance in some kind of rational way, "I saw duct tape with the word ABANDONED on her forehead, so I pulled it off!"

"I know her husband left her and the kids a couple of months ago," this other woman explained. "That's probably why it said ABANDONED on her head."

As you can imagine, the drama caught the attention of the entire table and created a buzz among the ladies. I tried my best to answer their questions without freaking anyone out, as most of them had very little understanding of the spirit world. Several minutes passed as the conversation continued. Eventually, the young lady got off the floor and struggled back to her seat next to me. I looked over at her, and this time I saw with my spirit the word DEPRESSION written on duct tape that was stuck to her head. With her permission, I ripped it off her forehead, and she went down on the floor again. This kind of scene repeated itself four times, until finally she was free from all her oppression. The last time she got off the floor, she was so full of joy that it inspired the other women at the table to ask for help.

We spent the next hour pulling invisible duct tape off their foreheads, too. It noted various afflictions like ABUSED, RAPED, CHRONIC FATIGUE and so forth. As we did this, some would crumple into a fetal position, weeping on the floor, while others would go into a spiritual trance for several minutes. It was wild!

My team and I spent three days in this spiritual vortex as Jesus guided person after person to us for restoration. Everywhere we went, people would stop us and ask for "prayer."

Hieroglyphics of the Spirit

This experience highlights several simple but profound insights into the spirit world that I want to explain to you so you can move more powerfully with the Lord. First of all, it is important to understand that God is not human. His first language is not English, Spanish or German, nor is it any other human language that you or I might speak, although it is not uncommon for Him to speak to us in our language. Yet one of the most common ways the Spirit speaks to us is in a language I call "Spiritual Hieroglyphics." Although we most often associate hieroglyphics with Egypt, the word *hieroglyphics* is Greek. *Hiero* means "holy," and *glyphics* means "marks" or "writings," so the two together mean "holy writings."

To be clear, I am not saying that God was inspiring the Egyptian cave writings or anything remotely similar. I am using the word *hieroglyphics* as a way to illustrate how the Holy Spirit often speaks to us in picture form. Let me cite an example from the Bible:

> Joseph had a dream, and when he told it to his brothers, they hated him even more. He said to them, "Please listen to this dream which I have had; for behold, we were binding sheaves in the field, and lo, my sheaf rose up and also stood erect; and behold, your sheaves gathered around and bowed down to my sheaf." Then his brothers said to him, "Are you actually going to reign over us? Or are you really going to rule over us?" So they hated him even more for his dreams and for his words.
>
> Now he had still another dream, and related it to his brothers, and said, "Lo, I have had still another dream; and behold, the sun and the moon and eleven stars were bowing down to me." He related it to his father and to his brothers; and his father rebuked him and said to him, "What is this dream that you have had? Shall I and your mother and your brothers actually come to bow ourselves down before you to the ground?"
>
> Genesis 37:5–10

Joseph's dreams illustrate both the hieroglyphic nature of the Spirit's language and the fact that Joseph's family understood how to decipher that dialect. Of course, the bowing sheaves represented his brothers, and later the sun, moon and bowing stars signified the entire family honoring Joe. In case you don't know the rest of the story, many years later Joseph became a ruler in Egypt, preceding a severe famine. He saved his family from destruction as they fled to Egypt to avoid starvation. Ultimately, his entire family bowed down to him in honor, just as the dreams foretold.

One of the main reasons so many people miss or ignore the voice of the Spirit is because they don't understand how to read "Spiritual Hieroglyphics." They are therefore unaware that God is actually talking to them. Personally, I learned how to be sensitive to the voice of the Spirit by missing it so many times. For instance, I would see a picture in my imagination such as a sword in someone's stomach, and I wouldn't say anything. A while later, I would find out that the person had a physical problem in the same location as the sword I saw in the spirit.

Over time, I started experimenting with such information by asking people questions. I would say, "I see a sword stuck in your stomach. Do you have any physical symptoms? Any pain, digestive issues or a diagnosis that would make sense of this vision?" Almost always, there would be a logical reason for the unusual vision. Over time, I grew more confident that my hieroglyphic visions were accurate depictions of real issues.

Interpreting the Secret Message

There are really two main types of visions. One kind is a vision of the mind, in which the Spirit projects an image (it could be a video or just a picture) onto the screen of your imagination (see Daniel 4:10). These images usually last less than three seconds, which of course is another reason people don't value them. You can usually "rerun the film" so to speak, by simply recalling the image back to your imagination.

The second kind I call an "open vision," which is very similar to the vision of the mind, except that you actually see it with your natural/physical eyes. Simply put, you close your eyes and the vision is gone, and when you open your eyes, it is there.

This inspires the question of how we know what visions mean. According to Daniel 2:28, ultimately God is the one who reveals mysteries and interprets His own spiritual language. That being said, it is clear through the Scriptures that the interpretation of visions and dreams is somewhat a spiritual skill that is at least partially learned through experience and training. In fact, this skill was often passed down in Bible days from generation to generation, as it was through Abraham's legacy. This is demonstrated in Abraham, his son Isaac, his grandson Jacob, and his great-grandson Joseph, including all of Joseph's brothers, who were guided by dreams and visions that they understood.

There are entire books dedicated to helping us understand how to interpret visions and dreams, so I will only share this brief overview on the subject. Here are four keys to understanding the languages of the Spirit:

1. It is important that you have a high value for hearing God, so that you pay close attention to these spiritual "episodes." The entire spirit world operates by faith, which is demonstrated through valuing the gift God has given you.

2. Faith in God is spelled R-I-S-K, meaning that you must be willing to take risks to see the Spirit move in power through you. These risks should not harm others, however, so it's probably unwise for you to start out by pulling swords of affliction out of politicians or strangers. Instead, cultivate a level of calculated risk at which you can learn and grow in the Spirit. I found that one of the best ways to begin living in the Spirit is to experiment with people with whom I have a relationship, by asking them a lot of "prophetic" questions. It's important to note here that the less experience you have, the more questions you should ask *before* making any kind of confident prophetic declaration to someone.

3. Pay attention to the prophetic interpretations that you get right, because a language pattern will begin to emerge from these positive experiences. A clear understanding of God's personal dialect (the way He speaks to you) will materialize in your life, and soon you will be reading His pictorial language accurately.

4. Sometimes it helps to describe a vision or image to the people you are ministering to and ask them what it means to them. Often, God will speak to you in *their* personal dialect instead of *yours*. For example, God gave me a certain number from the time I was young. It is God's secret code for me. Whenever someone uses that specific number, I know they are hearing from God for me! The number is meaningless to others, but to me it means, *Pay close attention to what this person tells you, as I am speaking to you through him [or her].*

We will talk more about interpreting the messages God is speaking to you, as well as discerning what's happening around you in the spiritual realm and what to do about it. The more experience you gain in these areas, the more you will increase your spiritual intelligence—your SQ—and the more clearly you will understand His voice and be able to act on what He is telling you.

In fact, at the end of the book I have included an assessment tool that will help you do just that—not only gauge where you are now with your SQ level, but also find out what you can do to increase it. Taking the *Spiritual Intelligence Quotient (SQ) Assessment* at the back will help you figure out the primary way (or ways) you and God tend to communicate, and will also provide you with specific action steps to take that will lead you into developing a higher level of SQ. By this point, you are far enough along in these pages to know what I mean by *spiritual intelligence* or SQ, so if you want to turn to the SQ assessment now and take it, go ahead.

Or you can keep reading now and wait until you reach the end of the book to take the assessment. Either way, I believe that when you do take it, your scores will help you analyze your personal SQ level. You will also learn about some ways you can increase your SQ level, so that day by day you can hear God's voice more clearly and act more confidently on what He is telling you—with supernatural results.

5

Led by the Spirit

Here is the big question: How do we actually cultivate a relationship with the God of the universe? Telling people that you talk to God often inspires a conversation around medication and mental illness. "Oh, you talk to God, do you? That's interesting. And what does He say to you?" These questions are asked with a "How long have you been hearing these voices?" kind of look. Furthermore, there are a lot of weird people out there announcing some crazy stuff in the name of God, so in some ways there is a legitimate fear of listening to the "voice" of God.

On the other hand, what kind of Creator would design a creature like humans, with our level of capacity for communication, and have no interaction with them, especially a Creator who calls Himself the Word of God? How can a God named the *Word* not talk to us? And if God is talking to us, then why do most people not hear Him, or at least not understand Him?

Let me start by quoting King Solomon: "It is the glory of God to conceal a matter, but the glory of kings is to search out a matter" (Proverbs 25:2). This verse teaches us that God hides things for us, not from us. You might ask, "Why does God hide things? Why doesn't He make His voice clear?"

That is a simple and yet complex question. First, knowledge is power, and God does not want the arrogant and prideful to be the powerful. He therefore conceals His voice in such a way that it is only revealed to the humble and the hungry.

Second, all of us are accountable for what we know, meaning that the more clearly we understand the will of God, the greater our capacity is to rebel, sin or disobey Him. The apostle James put it best: "Let not many of you become teachers, my brethren, knowing that as such we will incur a stricter judgment" (James 3:1). Obviously, revelation comes with accountability. The more we know, the greater our responsibility, and ultimately the more severe our judgment day will be. Moreover, when Jesus encountered demon-possessed people, they would often cry out, "You are the Son of God!" But Jesus would command them to shut up. I think He did this because He didn't want humans to understand the depth of their demise or the fact that they were actually killing their Creator, and He was lessening humanity's judgment by hiding a portion of His identity (see Mark 3:11; Luke 4:41).

You might be thinking, *If I knew the will of God, surely I would want to obey Him.* I hope so, but that is not God's experience with freewill agents. Long before He created humans in His own image, He created the angels. Angels were not created in the image of God, but they were given a free will, with which they could think for themselves (absent of God's intervention). These creatures live in the very presence of God, hearing His voice and experiencing Him personally. Yet Scripture tells us that one-third of the angels rebelled against God and attempted to dethrone Him. God defrocked those angels, and they were what I like to call "transmortified" into demons that were eventually thrown out of the third heaven with Satan, their rebel leader (see Revelation 12:9).

God helped solve the rebellion of His freewill agents with three distinctives: First, He made mankind in His own image and likeness, a mirror image of Himself (see Genesis 1:26–28). The Bible says,

"But we all, with unveiled face, beholding as in a mirror the glory of the Lord, are being transformed into the same image from glory to glory, just as from the Lord, the Spirit" (2 Corinthians 3:18). Second, He puts His Spirit in everyone who chooses to follow Him (unlike the demons who rebelled against Him). John wrote, "By this we know that we abide in Him and He in us, because He has given us of His Spirit" (1 John 4:13). And third, to those who allow His Spirit to live inside them and so house God, He gives the mind of Christ and His heart (see again 1 Corinthians 2:6–16). Remember, none of this takes away our free will, but it does reveal to us God's will in varying degrees.

Pruned with a Purpose

By now, it should have become clear that the level of our spiritual intelligence is determined by the depth of our relationship with our "Spirit Guide," who is the Holy Spirit. The Holy Spirit has been assigned to guide us into *all* truth (see John 16:13). In fact, Jesus said that "the Helper, the Holy Spirit, whom the Father will send in My name, He will teach you all things, and bring to your remembrance all that I said to you" (John 14:26). Yet the health of our relationship with the Spirit is largely predicated on our ability to obey God. Here is a rather long, yet profound passage of Scripture on the subject:

> I am the true vine, and My Father is the vinedresser. Every branch in me that does not bear fruit, He takes away; and every branch that bears fruit, He prunes it so that it may bear more fruit. You are already clean because of the word which I have spoken to you. Abide in Me, and I in you. As the branch cannot bear fruit of itself unless it abides in the vine, so neither can you unless you abide in Me. I am the vine, you are the branches; he who abides in Me and I in him, he bears much fruit, for apart from Me you can do nothing. If anyone does not abide in Me, he is thrown away as a branch and dries up; and they gather them, and cast them into the fire and they are burned. If

you abide in Me, and My words abide in you, ask whatever you wish, and it will be done for you. My Father is glorified by this, that you bear much fruit, and so prove to be My disciples. Just as the Father has loved Me, I have also loved you; abide in My love. If you keep My commandments, you will abide in My love; just as I have kept My Father's commandments and abide in His love. These things I have spoken to you so that My joy may be in you, and that your joy may be made full.

This is My commandment, that you love one another, just as I have loved you. Greater love has no one than this, that one lay down his life for his friends. You are My friends if you do what I command you. No longer do I call you slaves, for the slave does not know what his master is doing; but I have called you friends, for all things that I have heard from My Father I have made known to you. You did not choose Me but I chose you, and appointed you that you would go and bear fruit, and that your fruit would remain, so that whatever you ask of the Father in My name He may give to you.

John 15:1–16

Let's first unpack this parable, and then I will show you how it relates to hearing the voice of the Spirit. The parable reminds me of my uncle who had a small vineyard in the Napa Valley of California when I was a teenager. I used to work on his farm once in a while in the summer. I didn't really pay much attention to what I was doing in those days; I just hacked off the branches wherever my uncle instructed me to. But looking back now, I remember finding branches about twenty feet long, on which the first five feet had grapes, the next three feet had only leaves, and the last twelve feet of the same branches were just long sticks. I realize now that a vine, left unattended, will spend all its energy extending its branches longer, until it has no energy left to produce leaves, much less fruit. In other words, a grapevine becomes a stick tree if it gets overextended. If you don't prune the branch all the way back to its fruitfulness, then the vine's capacity to produce fruit will be siphoned off to grow sticks.

In this parable God is the farmer, Jesus is the vine, and we, of course, are the branches. What is profound here is that God uses His "word" to prune the branches, which is illuminated in the verse "You are already clean because of the word which I have spoken to you" (verse 3). The word *clean* here is the same Greek root word as *pruned*. In other words, God uses His "word" to prune us back to our place of fruitful revelation and obedience. He hacks off everything (the dead wood) that is overextended and is undermining our divine responsibility and derailing our destiny.

Jesus goes on to state the obvious: If a branch is disconnected from the vine, it cannot do anything like grow leaves or produce grapes. So there is an exhortation for us to stay connected and make an effort to have a vibrant, healthy, ongoing relationship with Jesus. One of the ways we can tell that people have a healthy relationship with God is that their weird and anti-biblical "revelation" gets pruned off.

But here is where the good stuff starts to happen. Jesus promised, "If you abide in Me, and My words abide in you, ask whatever you wish, and it will be done for you" (verse 7). I was so taken by this verse a few years ago that I actually started writing a book called *Wishful Thinking*. The idea that we could have *anything* we ask for is stunning . . . I mean, epic! I guess the challenge is that I don't know anyone living the dream, at least not to that level, and yet it is right there in the Good Book, and these are the words of Jesus, no less.

Here is the kicker: If we take Jesus at His word—"Whatever you ask in My name, that will I do" (John 14:13)—then we have to have a prunable relationship with Him in which we listen to Him and let Him cut off the things in our hearts and minds that He deems deadwood dangerous.

But wait, it gets even better. Jesus said, "You are My friends if you do what I command you. No longer do I call you slaves, for the slave does not know what his master is doing; but I have called you friends, for all things that I have heard from My Father I have made known to you" (verses 14–15). Once we learn to obey His commands, then we are promoted from slaves to friends. This relational transition from slave to friend opens the door for profound revelation in our lives. A slave only knows how to obey his master, but friends have a full-access pass to the voice of the Father!

My Journey

When I was a young believer (in spiritual maturity, not age), many people who had a deep relationship with God inspired me. I read several life-changing books, and of course the Bible, which created a hunger in me actually to know God. I wanted to have heavy revelations similar to the characters in the Bible, move in power like Jesus and hear the voice of the Spirit regularly. I decided to press into God every day by kneeling by my bed in the mornings before work and asking God for a word I could obey.

I was thinking God would give me some amazing prophetic word that would stun the world (or at least impress my family). So the first morning, I knelt down and listened anxiously. I heard, *Pick up the trash around Tops Market parking lot on your way home from work.*

What! Pick up trash? How could that be You, God? I complained. I drove past Tops Market on my way home that night, remembering the word I had heard that morning, but ignoring it. My family and I sat down for dinner and prayed for the meal. Suddenly, I heard this thundering Voice in my spirit: *You disobeyed me! Go pick up the trash I told you to pick up this morning!*

I excused myself, got up from the table and told my family I would be right back. (I didn't tell them I was going out to pick up trash. I didn't want them to think I had lost my marbles.) I quickly picked up all the garbage in the parking lot at Tops Market and went back home.

A couple of days later, on a Saturday morning, I was kneeling by my bed, waiting for my next assignment. I was feeling pretty spiritual, having congratulated myself for my big trash exploit. I was sure

I was ready for the next level of revelation. This time I heard, *Good job cleaning up the parking lot. I want you to spend the day picking up all the trash on the highway that goes through town.*

I was livid! *I own four businesses and have thirty employees. What are people going to think of me picking up garbage on the highway?* I protested. But there was no answer, no Voice and no conviction—just complete silence. I went to work thinking we would be so busy that I really wouldn't have time to clean up the road, but business was dead that morning. In fact, I don't think we had a single customer come into the store the first hour. I grabbed a large garbage can, stomped out the door and threw it in the back of my truck (which, by the way, had our big logo on the side). I picked up trash along both sides of the highway for eight long, grueling hours! I must have had a hundred people stop to ask what I was doing. Many even asked if they could help. Of course, I didn't dare tell anyone that I heard a Voice telling me to pick up trash. And I certainly didn't want anyone to help me, as I could only guess how that might delay my promotion.

I continued to pray every day on my knees by my bed. But I had a change of heart during my highway trash pick-up venture. I started to realize that I was going to have to do stupid stuff until I stopped having a stupid attitude, because God was trying to change me from the inside out. I felt convicted for the pride that had caused me to feel as though I were too important to pick up garbage. I asked God to forgive me for being more concerned about what people thought of me than I was about obeying Him. I vowed to do anything He asked of me from that day on.

Turn Aside

Moses encountered a burning bush in the wilderness that was not consumed, and when he turned aside to try to understand the phenomenon, God spoke to him from the bush. Burning bushes are common in the desert due to spontaneous combustion, so I think it is likely that Moses walked past that same bush for many days or even weeks before he turned aside to check it out. One of the most common reasons we don't hear God on any kind of regular basis is because we don't "turn aside" from our daily activities to hear Him. Jeremiah prophesied it like this: "You will seek Me and find Me when you search for Me with all your heart" (Jeremiah 29:13). The heart of the matter is really the matter of the heart. God wants us to value our relationship with Him, not treat Him like a cosmic bellhop or a casual friend.

If my friend calls me, I may see his name come up on my caller ID and think, *I'm not in the mood to talk to him today. I'll call him back later.* But if the president of the United States calls me, I will likely have quite a different response to him or her. I like the way Bobby Connor, a prophetic friend of mine, explains the situation: "We are too familiar with the God we hardly know." That's exactly right! The problem with having a full-access pass to the throne of God is that we often wind up in a casual relationship with Him. We treat God as we would a partner in a cohabiting relationship, instead of laying our lives down in covenant with Him.

A few years ago, I started waking up most nights at about 3:00 a.m. to conversations with the Spirit. Finally, after weeks of lost sleep, I asked God why He kept waking me up in the middle of the night. He said, *You are too busy for Me during the day!*

Yikes! I thought to myself. Guillermo Maldonado, an apostle of a megachurch in Florida, said at a conference that I attended, "Some men go to the gym every day to work out their body, but they don't pray ten minutes a day. They have a $100,000 body and a 10-cent spirit!" He went on to exhort the men, "Some men spend more time with their fantasy sports team than they do with their reality God!" His final prod was, "Many men know the stats of their sports team better than they know their Bible."

Although this is sort of blunt, it is also so true. Most of us spend an hour a day getting ready for work, making sure we look and smell good for people who couldn't care less, but we don't spend any time growing our inner man for God.

Voice Lessons

Speaking of the Good Shepherd, Jesus said of someone who is a shepherd, "The sheep follow him because they know his voice. A stranger they simply will not follow, but will flee from him, because they do not know the voice of strangers" (John 10:4–5). The Good Shepherd's sheep likewise know His voice and follow Him (although His lambs are still learning to hear the voice of the Master).

There is something simple but profound about learning to hear a person's voice. For example, let's say I want to teach you how to hear the voice of my wife, Kathy. I could remind you that Kathy is a woman, which would eliminate half the population of the earth. I could let you know she is Caucasian, in her sixties, born in California, and she speaks no foreign languages. If I gave you enough clues, I probably could eliminate 7 billion people alive on the planet today, leaving only about 800 million people for you to pick from. But the only way for you actually to know Kathy's voice is to hear her speak numerous times.

The same is true of the Holy Spirit. There is no way to read any book, including the Bible, and know the voice of God. The Bible does teach us about the nature of the Spirit, so like my illustration of Kathy, we can vet out the foreign or deceptive voices that might want to lead us astray. But there is no substitute, no shortcut and no end around actually spending time with God.

One of the best ways for you as a "lamb" (a new or inexperienced believer) to become familiar with the Lord's voice is to observe the response of the "sheep" around you (the mature Christians who know the voice of the Spirit) when you are in the same space with them. When I was a young Christian, we would put a person in a "hot seat" in the middle of the room and then give him or her prophetic words. After doing this for several months, I would notice that I often had the same prophetic word as the more experienced leaders for the person in the hot seat, and often even the same Scriptures. This was so reassuring! It really built up my faith in my ability to hear God.

Another method that aids in discerning the Lord's voice is to develop a group of believers who themselves are seeking to know God, and then to practice on each other. It can go something like this: "When you were a kid, was your bedroom yellow with purple trim? Did you have a stuffed animal bear you named Honey?" This is a simple way to grow your ability to learn to hear the Holy Spirit's voice without making a big mess. But it will be important to give each other very honest feedback. I refer to these kinds of exercises as "no mercy zones," meaning that we tell each other the truth. So if you really want to grow in the Spirit, you have to put on your Big Boy/Big Girl pants and be ready to dish out some great feedback and get some in return. It will take time to become a truly spiritually intelligent person, so be patient with yourself and keep your ears open.

People often ask me how often they can expect to hear from God, understanding that there were times in the Old Testament when the voice of the Lord was rare (see 1 Samuel 3:1). It is important to understand that the Holy Spirit came *on* people in the Old Testament, but He did not live *in* people. We are in a completely different epoch today. The apostle Paul wrote, "For all who are being led by the Spirit of God, these are sons of God" (Romans 8:14).

The connotation is that we are in an intimate relationship with the Holy Spirit in which we have access to His voice, His thoughts and His heart . . . all the time, any time. We are "filled" with the Spirit, meaning that we are His house and His container. In fact, we are the Spirit's clothes. He dresses Himself in us.

6

Pirates and Hackers

The voice of God is the catalyst for everything we do in life. But we have an enemy that is working overtime to distort the voice of God, disrupt the airwaves of communication and ultimately destroy us on every level—spirit, soul and body!

Internally, biological warfare is raging in us as sickness and disease battle our bodies in an attempt to annihilate us. These take up strategic positions within us, while our bodies fight back with an army of white blood cells equipped and commissioned to defeat them. Externally, murderers, thugs, thieves, rapists and ruthless criminals are plotting evil constantly against humanity.

The fact is, evil is everywhere, in every arena of life. A war between nations might be the ultimate manifestation of humans killing one another for the senseless sake of some twisted gain. I grew up in the sixties, when John Lennon famously sang his song "Give Peace a Chance." He and his wife, Yoko Ono, did two "Bed-Ins," which were weeklong peaceful protests against the Vietnam War from their own bedroom. I hate war, but the challenge with peace is that there is always some puppet of the "thief" who ultimately will not comply with it. Adolf Hitler, Joseph Stalin, Saddam Hussein and Mao

Zedong are just a few of the tyrants who literally killed millions of people under their rulership.

The truth is, most of the time real peace is only found in strength, preparation and vigilance, not in "Bed-Ins," sit-ins and peaceful protests. The reason may be obvious: Although most people are peaceful, there are some really evil people in the world who are dead set on destroying others. Much like a terrible virus or a deadly disease, these people are sick, decrepit, deadly tumors of society. You can't negotiate with terrorists; you can only stop them with greater force than their own.

Of course, Jesus can redeem anyone, so there is always hope. There is no industry, no people group, no religion and no nation, however, that is exempt from this evil force in the world. Think about it: Fewer than five decades ago, the computer was invented with the potential to solve literally millions of humanity's problems. The mere thought of each of us having full access to a genius in a box, with an answer to nearly any question we could ever ask, was wild—even stunning! But along with invention and innovation came hackers, pirates and thieves. Shortly after the very first software rolled out of production, a virus was created to destroy it.

Here is the way Jesus described this destructive dynamic: "The thief comes only to steal and kill and destroy" (John 10:10). The word *thief* is Jesus' descriptive term for Satan, the enemy of our souls. But then Jesus adds the hope: "I came that they may have life, and have it abundantly."

Spiritual Hackers

The spirit realm is likewise riddled with hackers and pirates who, for various reasons such as selfishness, deception or even downright wickedness, partner with the thief, Satan, to destroy people's lives. The unnerving truth is that spiritual hackers and pirates are highly deceptive, meaning they appear good or maybe even godly at times.

Jesus gave so many warnings like this one about people who are operating under the power of a delusional spirit: "For false Christs and false prophets will arise, and will show signs and wonders, in order to lead astray, if possible, the elect" (Mark 13:22).

Here is perhaps the most troubling of Jesus' warnings:

Beware of the false prophets, who come to you in sheep's clothing, but inwardly are ravenous wolves. You will know them by their fruits. Grapes are not gathered from thorn bushes nor figs from thistles, are they? So every good tree bears good fruit, but the bad tree bears bad fruit. A good tree cannot produce bad fruit, nor can a bad tree produce good fruit. Every tree that does not bear good fruit is cut down and thrown into the fire. So then, you will know them by their fruits.

Not everyone who says to Me, "Lord, Lord," will enter the kingdom of heaven, but he who does the will of My Father who is in heaven will enter. Many will say to Me on that day, "Lord, Lord, did we not prophesy in Your name, and in Your name cast out demons, and in Your name perform many miracles?" And then I will declare to them, "I never knew you; depart from me, you who practice lawlessness."

Matthew 7:15–23

The underlying challenge is that these people are operating in high levels of spiritual intelligence, but it is rooted in the thief and motivated by the wrong spirit. They operate in power, they perform signs and wonders, and they seem as innocent as sheep, but it is all just a show because they are wolves dressed up in sheep costumes.

Some of these people are pure evil and are very aware of what they are doing. Much like the Hitlers or Stalins of the world, they have a proactive, destructive agenda to kill, steal from and destroy people. Metaphorically speaking, they dress up as police officers to build trust with people so they can rob the bank of their lives. The apostle Peter showed no restraint when he described them: "But these, like unreasoning animals, born as creatures of instinct to be captured and killed, reviling where they have no knowledge, will in the destruction of those creatures also be destroyed" (2 Peter 2:12). (You might read that entire chapter of Peter's, if you dare!)

Yet there are others who are deceiving people, while they themselves are also deceived. They are working for the dark side, but they don't even know it. The apostle John warned, "Beloved, do not believe every spirit, but test the spirits to see whether they are from God, because many false prophets have gone out into the world" (1 John 4:1). On the surface, John mirrors Jesus' warnings about false prophets. Yet on deeper examination, there is a distinct difference, in that John is warning *believers* to beware of becoming false prophets by believing the wrong spirit. John opens the door to a completely different dialogue about deceivers by pointing out that some well-meaning people are actually unknowingly working for Satan.

I find among believers two common responses to these cautions. Either they blow through the warning signs of deception like a drunken madman with a death wish speeding through stop signs, or they avoid spiritual intelligence altogether, concluding that the risks are too great. Neither one of these is a wise choice for us.

Evil and Good

Think about it this way: The power of the new age movement is rooted in deception, but it often looks like the works of God. This reminds me of Moses' confrontation with Pharaoh over letting God's people go. Aaron, Moses' right-hand guy, threw down his staff and it became a snake. So the sorcerers threw down their staffs, and those became two snakes. Aaron's snake ate the sorcerers' snakes, which is kind of cool.

Moses and Aaron were not duplicating the sorcerers' miracles; the sorcerers were duplicating theirs! Yet the confusing thing is that the miracles looked identical; their staffs turned into snakes and so forth (see Exodus 7–8 for the whole story). The point is that although the supernatural acts performed by new age people may be identical to God's, the thief is still the one pulling their puppet strings.

A New Testament example of this is the slave girl who had a spirit of divination in the book of Acts. The girl followed Paul around for days, yelling, "These men are bond-servants of the Most High God, who are proclaiming to you the way of salvation" (Acts 16:17). Greatly annoyed, Paul finally cast the evil spirit out of her (see verse 18).

Did you notice that the spirit of divination was telling the truth about Paul? In other words, sometimes psychics, sorcerers, palm readers and astrologers get the information right, but the source is still bent on deception because the thief is lurking with evil intent in the background.

Reacting in Fear

The solution for many believers today is to abandon spiritual intelligence, miracles and supernatural acts, which ultimately plays right into the hands of the devil. Then powerless believers are preaching a powerless gospel to a people in bondage to a powerful thief.

From some people's perspective, all prophets today are false because, in their minds anyway, there is no such thing as modern-day prophets. Furthermore, all miracles today are false because the only last days' miracles are the ones the devil does to deceive people. If these things were true, Jesus would have warned us that all miracles and all prophets in the last days would be false. *But He didn't!* In fact, the reason why false prophets are so deceptive is that there are real ones. The reason why false signs are so deceptive is that there are real ones. The reason why false healings are so deceptive is that there are real ones. I could go on, but you get the point. If someone posed as a police officer to win your trust, the power of his cover is that there are real cops. If real police uniforms are blue, the poser certainly wouldn't want to wear a red one, because he would be trying to fit in. If miracles, signs, wonders and supernatural occurrences were not normal for believers, posers would not be able to hide.

The truth is that Jesus commissioned us to root out posers and demonstrate the superior power of the Kingdom of God. Believers are commissioned to be the white blood cells of the world! We are anointed, equipped and deployed to "destroy the works of the devil" and bring God's authentic goodness everywhere we go. If we abandon spiritual intelligence, then the pharaohs of the world will be left to their wicked devices, and the nations will be discipled by the thief.

Unusual Doesn't Mean Unbiblical

To the dismay of some modern theologians, the Bible is filled with acts of the Holy Spirit that can seem strange, new age or even cult-like. One case in point is trances. The only trances mentioned in the Bible are Holy Spirit trances. Peter fell into a trance in Acts 10:10 and was directed to take the Good News to the Gentiles. The apostle Paul fell into a trance in Acts 22:17 and was told to get out of Jerusalem to avoid harm. There is no mention of demonic trances in the entire Bible (although there certainly is such a thing). Yet some twenty-first-century believers are convinced that these experiences are always demonic. Read your Bible, people!

Let me make it clear that I am not advocating that people should make an effort to fall into trances. It seems clear that biblical trances happen spontaneously. Although the apostle Paul instructed us to "pursue love, yet desire earnestly spiritual gifts, but especially that you may prophesy" (1 Corinthians 14:1), there is no instruction about desiring or pursuing trances.

The book of Acts is filled with unusual yet powerful stories of God moving on or through His people. There were those who were intoxicated by the Holy Spirit and spoke in tongues. Some experienced angel-assisted jailbreaks. Paul blinded a guy named Bar-Jesus. The stories go on and on—deliverances, prophecies, prophets, Philip caught up by the Spirit and translated to another city, dead-raisings, the sick healed, miracles . . . it's all there. What's exciting is that Jesus invited us to participate in the Holy Spirit's acts: "Truly, truly, I say to you, he who believes in Me, the works that I do, he will do also; and greater works than these he will do; because I go to the Father" (John 14:12). He also said, "These signs will accompany those who have believed: in My name they will cast out demons, they will speak with new tongues; they will pick up serpents, and if they drink any deadly poison, it will not hurt them; they will lay hands on the sick, and they will recover" (Mark 16:17–18; I get that people don't like the snake and poison thing, but it's in the Bible!). Yet many believers refuse to heal the sick and cast out demons.

I want to reiterate here that there are false healers, just as there are false teachers, false prophets, false signs, false wonders and false believers. Much like Moses' encounter with Pharaoh's sorcerers, the false is unleashed on the world to compete with the real, authentic power of God. This is a demonic military strategy to confuse people, dilute the truth and resist God's purposes in people's lives.

One thing is for sure, however. The thief's power is limited, as demonstrated by the fact that Moses and Aaron displayed ten miracles to force Pharaoh to let God's people go, whereas the sorcerers were only able to duplicate three of them (generating snakes from their staffs, turning water to blood and causing frogs to cover the land). It seems funny to me that the magicians were intensifying the plagues to demonstrate to their boss that they could do miracles, too. Dumb and dumber, I'd say! I love this part of the story:

> Aaron stretched out his hand with his staff, and struck the dust of the earth, and there were gnats on man and beast. All the dust of the earth became gnats through all the land of Egypt. The magicians tried with their secret arts to bring forth gnats, but they could not;

so there were gnats on man and beast. Then the magicians said to Pharaoh, "This is the finger of God."

Exodus 8:17–19

The way forward is deeper in! We cannot withdraw in the midst of the battle. We have to be like Moses and Aaron, and turn it up another notch. Jesus proclaimed, "I have given you authority to tread on serpents and scorpions, and over all the power of the enemy, and nothing will injure you" (Luke 10:19). I like the descriptive names Jesus gives to the demonic spirits—serpents and scorpions. It reveals their divisive nature, their illusive style and their poisonous posture. The question is, Does the thief have power? The answer is yes, but believers have more power, and they have *all* authority over every demonic enemy, meaning Satan has no authority.

New Covenant—More Power

Thankfully, we live in the New Covenant, so we no longer need to punish the pharaohs of the world with plagues. But Jesus clearly articulated the fact that we still need power, as Moses and Aaron did, to fulfill our divine mission. He instructed His disciples "not to leave Jerusalem," but to wait because "you will receive power when the Holy Spirit has come upon you; and you shall be My witnesses" (Acts 1:4, 8). We need the Holy Spirit, just as they did.

Of course, it's true that learning to live in the Spirit and be led by the Spirit can be messy. Spiritual intelligence comes at a cost, and we will make many mistakes as we learn and grow in the Lord—that's for sure. Yet, personally, I would rather take the risk of living out God's power instead of reducing my experience in the Spirit down to something I can control.

Again, the way out of this demonic mess is deeper in. If Moses and Aaron had quit after demonstrating a couple of miracles to the most powerful king of the earth of their time, they would have reduced history to hundreds of more years of Israelite bondage. But they didn't. They pushed past their fears and pressed in for more miracles. They kept taking it higher, until the sorcerers and magicians were humiliated and finally that stubborn, stiff-necked, baby-killing tyrant lost his grip on God's people. The Israelites left Egypt loaded down with wealth, a payment for four hundred years of slavery.

This is the power of SQ, and the privilege of all those who walk in the Spirit. We can go deeper in and take it higher and win, yet we also have to stay aware of pirates, hackers and deceivers as we learn and grow in the Spirit. The more we move in the power of the Spirit, the greater threat we will be to the kingdom of darkness. It is therefore important that we understand the devious ways of the devil, so that we can stay free of his devices and destroy his works.

7

Living from Heaven toward Earth

You may be wondering how to push past spiritual pirates, hackers and deceivers so that you can operate in true SQ, which is rooted in God's Kingdom of light. I propose that your spiritual seat, or the position from which you rule and think, will determine your ultimate success. Let me tell you about a time when I saw this play out in my life.

Recently, some of us from the Bethel Leadership Team were invited to a gathering at a prestigious think tank in Washington, D.C., to dialogue about some of America's toughest problems. The sessions were each about an hour long, beginning at 9:00 a.m. and lasting deep into the night, for two days. My team had high expectations for the gathering as we looked forward to interacting with forty of some of the brightest minds of our time. The day began with a PowerPoint presentation of several of the unhealthiest trends happening in our country. Homelessness, poverty, immorality, racism and the deconstruction of the family unit were just a few of the subjects presented at the forum. The first presenter was quite engaging, which produced a lot of expectation in us for the sessions to follow. But unfortunately, as the day progressed, virtually all we talked about were symptomatic cures, first-heaven perspectives (I'll explain that in a minute) and reactionary objectives.

Halfway through the first day, my team was ready to leave. We were all surprised that a gathering of believers this prestigious was not uncovering more heavenly insights into the earth's most destructive challenges. It was not that the proposed remedies were wrong or even dumb, but they lacked divine insight and any real understanding of our authority in the Spirit. In fact, these core perspectives were defensive survival techniques spoken in secret by people who viewed themselves as victims of the culture. Personally, I was vacillating between frustrated and irritated all day.

Finally, my team huddled up and decided to see if we could inspire our new friends to do some revelatory thinking. We began by asking the presenters some intriguing questions in the main sessions:

- How does our third-heaven seat affect our first-heaven situations? (Again, I'll explain those terms in a moment.)
- What does it look like to disciple nations (Matthew 28:19)?
- If the highest heavens belong to the Lord, but God gave the earth to the sons of men, what level of authority do we have to lead people well?
- Why does the Lord's Prayer include "Your Kingdom come . . . on earth as it is in heaven" (Matthew 6:10)?
- Why does the Bible say that our struggle is not against flesh and blood, but against demonic forces in heavenly places (Ephesians 6:12)?
- Do we as believers have any advantage over those who don't know God in our ability to be cultural architects and shape people's mindsets?

As you might imagine, this opened up an entirely different dialogue as we began to introduce spiritual intelligence manifested through third-heaven perspectives to our new friends. We said, "We like the charts, surveys and PowerPoint perspectives of our first-heaven challenges. But you actually can't solve first-heaven symptoms with first-heaven solutions, because the second heaven is actually creating the root issues. We must have third-heaven resolutions to these first-heaven issues, or we relegate our world to second-heaven domination!"

By now, you might be joining the gathering's attendees in displaying that "deer in the headlights" look that seemed to be in vogue that day. Let me explain these powerful truths a little further. The Bible teaches us that there are three heavens. Take a look at the following verses and their explanations:

- First heaven: "In the beginning God created the *heavens and the earth*" (Genesis 1:1, emphasis added). This is the visible world, the dimension that our five senses are acutely tuned in to, the natural realm that we are all aware of and interact with on a daily basis.

- Second heaven: "Our struggle is not against flesh and blood, but against the rulers, against the powers, against the world forces of this darkness, against the spiritual forces of wickedness in the *heavenly places*" (Ephesians 6:12, emphasis added). Notice the apostle Paul said that there are evil forces in *heavenly places*. Let's be clear: There are no demonic, satanic or evil forces in God's heaven. Thus, we call this realm from which Satan rules the second heaven.

- Third heaven: "I know a man in Christ who fourteen years ago—whether in the body I do not know, or out of the body I do not know, God knows—such a man was caught up to the *third heaven*. And I know how such a man—whether in the body or apart from the body I do not know, God knows—was caught up into Paradise and heard inexpressible words, which a man is not permitted to speak"

79

(2 Corinthians 12:2–4, emphasis added). Paul the apostle reveals through his own spiritual experience that there is a *third heaven* two levels above our earthly experience and one level above the satanic realm.

Where You Sit Matters

Now let me take you on a third-heaven, revelatory journey through some of the most powerful Scriptures ever inspired by the Holy Spirit. Please read this slowly, and let's consider the life-changing—maybe even world-changing—impact of these profound passages. Paul writes,

> I pray that the eyes of your heart may be enlightened, so that you will know what is the hope of His calling, what are the riches of the glory of His inheritance in the saints, and what is the surpassing greatness of His power toward us who believe. These are in accordance with the working of the strength of His might which He brought about in Christ, when He raised Him from the dead and seated Him at His right hand in the heavenly places, far above all rule and authority and power and dominion, and every name that is named, not only in this age but also in the one to come. And He put all things in subjection under His feet, and gave Him as head over all things to the church, which is His body, the fullness of Him who fills all in all.
>
> Ephesians 1:18–23

The first line makes my mind explode with possibility. Paul is literally praying the key theme of this book—that our hearts would be enlightened. The English word *enlighten* in this passage is translated from the Greek word *photizo*. We get our English word *photosynthesis* from this Greek word, which describes the process plants use to convert light energy to chemical energy to fuel the organisms' activity. Paul is praying that God's light would *photizo* in our hearts, or maybe more clearly, that His light would fuel us—converting light to revelation.

This is the foundation of spiritual intelligence, the very essence of the impact of the Light of the world on humanity—not just that we can *see*, but that we *become* the essence of His revelation. This is how we become "the light of the world" (see Matthew 5:14). His light works in us, but God's divine purpose is that it also works *through* us. Isaiah prophesied this *photizo* dynamic some five hundred years before Christ was born:

> Arise, shine; for your light has come, and the glory of the LORD has risen upon you. For behold, darkness will cover the earth and deep darkness the peoples; but the LORD will rise upon you and His glory will appear upon you. Nations will come to your light, and kings to the brightness of your rising.
>
> Isaiah 60:1–3

We are commanded to arise and shine. It is important to note in this context that the prophet does not say "arise and reflect." He says *shine*.

"Kris, what's the point here?" you ask. God is not just revealing truth to us; He is putting the "Spirit of revelation" in us so that we become co-revealers of truth. He is giving us spiritual intelligence in a way that will attract the world.

In Paul's prayer for revelation, which we just read in Ephesians 1, he prays that we would gain three specific insights:

1. "what is the hope of His calling" (verse 18)
2. "what are the riches of the glory of His inheritance in the saints" (verse 18)
3. "what is the surpassing greatness of His power toward us who believe" (verse 19)

Paul said these three revelations are "in accordance with" (verse 19). In other words, in order to understand the revelation of the first three (our *calling, inheritance* and *power*), we must understand that they are rooted in the list of powerful truths that follows them. These truths are to the spirit world what the laws of physics are to the natural world. It is simply impossible to understand the power of the Gospel and the authority of the believer in Christ without truly grasping the full revelation of this declaration. Here are the four truths that follow, which the three revelations are rooted in:

1. "The working of the strength of His might, which He brought about in Christ, when He raised Him from the dead" (verses 19–20).

   It isn't just that God raised Jesus from the dead, as Jesus was not the first one to be raised from the dead (consider Lazarus, for instance). It is the fact that when God raised Jesus from the dead, we believers *all* rose with Him. This is "the strength of His might," the profound truth that changed our lives forever.

2. The Father "seated Him at His right hand in the heavenly places, far above all rule and authority and power and dominion, and every name that is named, not only in this age but also in the one to come" (verses 20–21).

   Our heavenly Father positioned Jesus "*far above all* rule and authority and power and dominion." If we were ever to discover life on another planet, Jesus would still be in charge of it. If there are parallel universes, realms or any other strange creature living in some dimension that we can't even imagine, they will all be in submission to Jesus Christ. I know, I know, it all seems so weird! Yet when I read in the book of Revelation about God's strange "pets" that hang out around His throne, I think anything is possible.

3. "He put all things in subjection under His feet" (verse 22).

   In other words, the most insignificant believer in the Body of Christ still has authority over the most powerful evil principality in the cosmos!

4. He "gave Him as head over all things to the church, which is His body, the fullness of Him who fills all in all" (verse 22–23).

This intense demonstration of our identity in God stands on the shoulders of the truth that everything is under Jesus' feet and He is in charge. Furthermore, God "raised us up with Him, and seated us with Him in the heavenly places in Christ Jesus, so that in the ages to come He might show the surpassing riches of His grace in kindness toward us in Christ Jesus" (Ephesians 2:6–7; see verses 1–7). This reality, which is without question, should inspire us to live without fear and with a conviction that all darkness, opposition and spiritual oppression are defeated in Jesus.

Divine Fusion

Now, let's pull this all together and see if we can grasp the earthly ramifications of these amazing truths. Incredibly, the Lord has invited us to live from our heavenly throne toward our earthly dwelling so that we can profoundly shift the course of history toward His prosperous Kingdom.

We believers are not victims or helpless weaklings, hiding in the corner somewhere, hoping the devil doesn't destroy us. Nor are we a subservient subculture suffering under the power of worldly people who want to shove their perverted, poisonous and pretentious deceptions down our throats.

Instead, we are victors, with third-heaven authority over the devil's second-heaven devices. We are God's "solutionaries," commissioned to take third-heaven revelation and solve earth's first-heaven challenges with it.

This is "the hope of His calling," "the riches of the glory of His inheritance in the saints" and "the surpassing greatness of His power toward us who believe." This is it—you are blessed, glorious and powerful, the light of the world, the hope of the nations, Christ's answer to the world's problems!

The Problem

So many Christians live reactively from earth toward heaven, instead of living from heaven toward earth. They feel powerless most of their lives. Think about how these three heavens represent levels of power—the first heaven having the power of mere humanity, the second heaven having the power of the disruptive devil and his defunct cavalry of demons, and the third heaven carrying the authority and power of God Himself. If we abandon our third-heaven seat, then the human race becomes subject to the second heaven.

A lack of understanding of our authority in Christ has caused us as believers to relinquish to the devil our divine call to disciple nations. In doing so, we have sublet our authority to a de-authorized devil and have consequently commissioned the second heaven to rule the world. Paul went on to describe the war we wage against a defeated but determined foe. Let's revisit Ephesians 6:12 and dissect the destructive elements it talks about, so we can defeat them on our terms: "Our struggle is not against flesh and blood, but against the *rulers*, against the *powers*, against *the world forces of this darkness*, against the *spiritual forces of wickedness* in the heavenly places" (emphasis added).

The word *rulers* in this passage is revealing and unnerving. It is the Greek word *arche*, meaning "origins," "beginnings" and/or "elementary teachings." Before we go on from here, it is important to understand that evil spirits are named by the influence they have on humanity. For example, in Mark 9:14–29 Jesus encountered a father with a demonized son who was mute. Jesus said, "Deaf and dumb spirit, I command you, come out of him," and immediately the boy was restored to perfect health (verse 25 NKJV).

It is also important to note that not all demons have the same level of authority. In fact, the spirit realm operates much like the hierarchy of an army, with some spirits operating as soldiers warring in individual, one-on-one battles, while other spirits are high-ranking generals governing entire cities with their influence. Jesus explained it like this:

> Now when the unclean spirit goes out of a man, it passes through waterless places seeking rest, and does not find it. Then it says, "I will return to my house from which I came"; and when it comes, it finds it unoccupied, swept, and put in order. Then it goes and takes along with it *seven other spirits more wicked than itself*, and they go in and live there; and the last state of that man becomes worse than the first.
>
> Matthew 12:43–45, emphasis added

With that being said, and knowing that these spirits Paul is speaking about are not just demons, but are ruling spirits (generals in the second heaven), we now have some understanding of the impact that different principalities are assigned to have on the world. For example, Satan has commissioned a spirit called "Origin" to redefine the origins of creation. Here are a few examples of the way this demonic prince is working to question and pervert the origins God designed into creation:

- Are you really created in the image of God, or are you just an evolutionized ape? (Questioning the origin of mankind.)
- Is that a baby, or is it just a fetus? (Questioning the origin or beginning point of life.)
- Are you really a boy, or maybe you're a girl? (Questioning the origin, or original and distinctly different design, of males and females.)
- Were you really designed to marry the opposite sex, or maybe you can choose whatever sex you want to marry? (Questioning and bringing confusion about the origin of family.)

You can often tell when "Origin" (this principality that is attempting to redefine creation) is involved in a person's thinking, because even really smart people will believe something ridiculous and swear it is true. Science, logic and reason are no match for an evil *prince* because demonic revelation does not originate in the mind, but in the spirit realm.

Look at this short list of questions and think about the evil yet profound impact the second heaven is having on society. Many people have no idea that life has purpose anymore, because they have been deceived into believing that they are not sons and daughters of God, but rather, they are just evolved amoebas or smart chimps. The suicide epidemic is at a level we have never before experienced in the history of the world, and I believe this assault on us as God's creation has something to do with it.*

Many mothers are deceived into believing that they are pregnant with a fetus who is not human. This deception has fueled the worst holocaust ever! In fact, in the United States alone we have killed at least one hundred times more infants than Hitler gassed in the killing chambers of Nazi Germany. Mothers and fathers are standing in line to pay for the destruction of their own children. Abortion has become a major factor in the depopulation of more than thirty countries.†

Gender dysphoria—a girl who is convinced she is a boy or a boy who believes he is a girl—is now embraced as normal. In California and several other states (and other nations), people are attempting to make it illegal for a teacher or a therapist to do anything but affirm a person's chosen gender, including children. Already, young girls are having their breasts removed and are taking hormone treatments to try to "transition" into men. Boys are having their penises removed and are having a pseudo vagina created, along with taking hormone treatments to become women. Of course, it is all cosmetic change. Gender is genetic and cannot actually be altered.

---

* Hannah Ritchie, Max Roser, and Esteban Ortiz-Ospina, "Suicide," *Our World in Data*, 2020, https://ourworldindata.org/suicide.

† Guttmacher Institute, "Induced Abortion Worldwide," March 2018, https://www.guttmacher.org/fact-sheet/induced-abortion-worldwide.

But wait, it gets even crazier! Transgender women (women who are biologically men) are now competing against genetic women in sports and beating them. That's no surprise since men are typically about 10 percent stronger and 15 percent faster than women.‡ What is surprising is that genetic men are allowed to compete on these terms.

Those who are part of the LGBTQ movement have worked hard to convince society that there is no difference between mommies and daddies, so it is therefore normal for children to have two moms or two dads. Moms and dads are interchangeable, they argue. In fact, in 2019 California introduced "genderless curriculum" into the public school system, beginning at age five. There is a lot of pressure in the California public schools for educators not to use the pronouns *he* and *she*, and they must now only use the words *us*, *them* or *they*. The question is, Why do really smart people think all of this is rational? Because they are under the influence of the principality called "Origin," who is deceiving an entire generation.

This is the fruit of deserting our heavenly seat and going AWOL from our third-heaven responsibility. It is therefore urgent—but more than just urgent, it is critical—but much more than critical, it is crucial—that we take our rightful seat in the heavenlies and begin to *lead*. We must begin leading with nobility, honor and divine wisdom, which ultimately equals spiritual intelligence.

Wisdom from Another World

Speaking of third-heaven revelation and divine wisdom, the apostle Paul wrote this:

> To me, the very least of all saints, this grace was given, to preach to the Gentiles the unfathomable riches of Christ, and to bring to light

‡ A. E. Miller, J. D. MacDougall, M. A. Tarnopolsky, and D. G. Sale, "Gender differences in strength and muscle fiber characteristics," *European Journal of Applied Physiology and Occupational Physiology*, PubMed: US National Library of Medicine, 1993, www.ncbi .nlm.nih.gov/pubmed/8477683.

what is the administration of the mystery which for ages has been hidden in God who created all things; so that the manifold wisdom of God might now be made known through the church to the rulers and the authorities in the heavenly places.

Ephesians 3:8–10

We have been commissioned, called and equipped to display the "manifold wisdom of God" to *rulers* and *authorities* in heavenly places. This word *rulers* is the same Greek word we spoke of earlier—*arche*, meaning "origins." I find it fascinating that we (Jesus people) are commissioned to teach those in the heavenly realm about the manifold wisdom of God. You might be asking yourself why or even how we would teach demonic princes about God's divine wisdom. Yet Paul is not talking about teaching demonic princes here; he is referring to angelic principalities who abide in the third heaven and are assigned to co-labor with us in our divine mission.

The Symptoms of Your Seat

If you are one of those practical people, I can hear you groaning by now, *How do I know if I'm living from earth or from heaven?* Here are seven symptoms that you are living from *earth* toward *heaven*:

1. You worry a lot.
2. You feel like a powerless victim, and you have a big devil and a little God.
3. You don't think you have anything to contribute to making the world a better place.
4. You're convinced that every year the world is getting worse.
5. All your prayers are in reaction to a bad circumstance.
6. You have no vision for the future.
7. You struggle with low self-esteem and a poverty mentality.

Here are seven symptoms that you are living from *heaven* toward *earth*:

1. You believe God can do the impossible, and you think like He does.

2. You live with a one-hundred-year vision and plan to leave a legacy to your children's children.

3. The world's troubles only serve to challenge you to think big and bring God's ideas to the table.

4. You view devil encounters as a compliment to the fact that you are doing something worth resisting, and you see these encounters as opportunities to win.

5. You know you are a son or daughter of the King; therefore, you carry yourself like royalty.

6. The commission to disciple nations positively affects your prayer life as you shape history on your knees.

7. You look for God's perspective on current events, and you refuse to let the media or a political or religious spirit shape your mindset or cloud your worldview.

It is time to step up into your heavenly seat, if that is not where you are living from already. Jesus is waiting for you. He has made a place for you on the throne. He is excited for you to experience using the authority He purchased for you on the cross!

8

The Gift of Discernment

In some ways, wars are fought in the physical realm—guns blazing and bombs blasting. Yet other times, a war is won or lost in the secret intelligence that is discovered before the troops are ever deployed.

For example, the Battle of Midway was a decisive naval battle fought in World War II's Pacific theater in June 1942, six months after the attack on Pearl Harbor. The U.S. Navy repelled an attack by the Imperial Japanese Navy near Midway Atoll and inflicted heavy damage on the opposing fleet. One military historian, John Keegan, called it "the most stunning and decisive blow in the history of naval warfare."*

The Midway attack was Japan's attempt to eliminate the United States as a strategic power in the Pacific. The hope was that another demoralizing defeat like Pearl Harbor would force the U.S. to capitulate, giving the Imperial Fleet dominance in the Pacific Ocean. Luring American aircraft carriers into a trap at Midway was part of that strategy. But a team of American cryptographers was able

* This quote and the surrounding information are taken from *Wikipedia*, s.v. "Battle of Midway," last modified March 16, 2020, https://en.wikipedia.org/wiki/Battle_of_Midway.

to decode information that revealed the date and location of the coming attack, so the U.S. Navy prepared its own ambush based on that intelligence. As a result, the Japanese fleet lost four of its carriers and a heavy cruiser. The Americans prevailed in the battle and ultimately went on to win the war.

Spiritual Cryptographers

Much like the Battle of Midway, in which an opposing navy plotted secretly to destroy the American fleet, the entire world is in an invisible war right now that most people don't even know about. Part of the challenge lies in the fact that Westerners often relate to Satan, demons and principalities as if they are fictional characters like Santa Claus and the Easter Bunny. They really have no grid, much less an understanding, of these entities, and thus they often become victims of the invisible realm.

That's right—as weird as it may sound, these entities are affecting our daily lives, our relationships, our health and our prosperity. Yet unlike the American naval fleet, many people have no idea that they are being lured right into a strategic battle designed to steal from, kill and destroy them. Their ignorance has allowed the demonic realm literally to hide in plain sight. The truth is, in order to live a prosperous and successful life, we *must* become spiritual cryptographers who understand that we are in a real battle. Then we have to decode the battle plans of our enemies so we can defeat them.

A movie titled *Midway* came out in 2019 dramatizing the historic Battle of Midway and the important part secret intelligence played in it. The producers did a great job of revealing how the cryptologist who dissected the intelligence came to a practical conclusion. The movie focuses on the story of Edwin Layton, the naval combat intelligence officer in charge of the team of cryptologists. He first warns Admiral Nimitz about the possibility of an attack on Pearl

Harbor, but the admiral ignores him. All the navy brass also think Layton is crazy. But soon, as ships at Pearl Harbor burn in the background, Admiral Nimitz and Layton have a passionate dialogue in which the admiral ends with something like, "Never let me ignore your advice again!"

Layton's team then decrypts intelligence that reveals there will be another attack, this time at Midway. Another heated conversation takes place in which the admiral tells Layton he is convinced the Japanese will attack somewhere else. Unmoved, Layton assures him the attack will be at Midway and reminds him of their previous exchange about his advice never being ignored again.

Unconvinced, Admiral Nimitz demands to know how Layton and his cryptographers could possibly know that the attack will take place at Midway, especially since Midway has not yet been named specifically in any of the intercepted messages.

Joseph Rochefort, one of Layton's team members, answers the admiral, "Sir, imagine that you're throwing a wedding. And maybe I've never seen the invitation, but I hear from the caterers that they have an event on a certain date. The flower guy is buying up all the roses on the island. The best band is booked. That's what signal intelligence can give you. Clues. Not a definitive answer."

Layton adds again, "Sir, after Pearl, you told me to stick to my guns. I swear to you, Joe's right about this."* And he was.

Like the American cryptologists demonstrated, so much of spiritual intelligence is not only learning to decode clues, but also having the divine insight to solve the riddle. The wisest king in the world unpacked this theme in the book of Proverbs when he revealed his purpose for writing that book: "To understand a proverb and a figure, the words of the wise and their riddles" (Proverbs 1:6).

In other words, God wants us to understand riddles, solve complex situations and reveal hidden mysteries. To become spiritual

---

* *Midway*, directed by Roland Emmerich, Summit Entertainment/Lionsgate, 2019.

cryptographers who unlock riddles, we must therefore understand *how* the spirit world actually works, and what it is we are dealing with—or maybe more importantly, *who it is*, so that we can navigate the pros and cons of this celestial dimension.

At the Last Minute

That being said, let me share a story with you that demonstrates the dangers and conquests of the spirit world. A few years ago, I got into a car with a friend of mine whom I have known for several years. Something crazy happened as soon as we pulled away from the curb. I suddenly had this overwhelming *feeling* that I wanted to kill myself! I struggled to figure out what the heck—or maybe more appropriately, what the "hell" was going on. I had never been suicidal, and I felt fine before getting into the car.

Still trying to shake the emotion, I looked over to see if my friend might be feeling it, too. Instantly, a picture emerged in my mind of her hanging herself. What made the situation even more confusing was that I knew she was a very stable person, so it didn't make any sense. To make matters worse, the ride was short. I wasn't sure what to do, but hastily I decided to take a risk and go for it.

"Mary (not her real name), are you all right?" I inquired.

"Why do you ask?" she countered.

"Well, actually, I had a weird feeling when I got in the car that I wanted to kill myself, and then I closed my eyes and saw a strange vision. You were hanging by a rope," I said cautiously.

Looking at me as if she had seen a ghost, Mary suddenly started gasping for air and weeping uncontrollably. "I've had this overwhelming urge to kill myself—to die—for six months!" she blurted out. "Last night it got so unbearable . . . so strong . . . that I couldn't take it! I couldn't stand it anymore! I tied a rope around my neck and was getting ready to jump. But right before I . . . before I jumped, a Voice in my mind said, *Tomorrow, I am going to deliver you!*"

While she was pouring out her heart, I saw a vision in my mind of me commanding the *spirit of suicide* to leave her. I said, "I believe I'm supposed to command this spirit of suicide to leave you right now. Shall I do it?"

"*Yes!*" she shouted. "Just make this thing leave me *alone!*"

"Okay, hang on to the steering wheel with both hands," I instructed. (I have to admit that casting a demon out of her while she was driving seemed like a really bad idea, but I was already committed).

I proclaimed, "You spirit of suicide, leave this woman now, *in Jesus' name!*"

Mary jerked for a second, coughed and then drove on in silence, while tears streamed down her face. A minute later we arrived at our destination and I opened the door and got out. Then I leaned back in and asked, "Are you okay?"

Still weeping, she replied, "Yes!" In a quiet voice she added, "It's gone—completely gone!"

I saw Mary the next day and was anxious to hear how she was doing. Her face said it all; she was glowing!

Before I could ask, she began to thank me profusely. "I owe you my life," she began. "If it weren't for you, I would be dead. That evil thing left me, and I'm completely free!"

Cohabiting the Planet

Mary's story demonstrates so well that we live on a planet dramatically infected and affected by an invisible world full of unseen beings living among us. The truth is, we don't inhabit this planet. Instead, we cohabit the earth with these other beings that live in another realm or exist in something like a different frequency. Much like radio or television waves that are invisible to our five senses, yet perceptible with the right equipment, this spirit world is also (most often) undetectable by our natural senses, but very observable through our spiritual senses.

Furthermore, at least one-third of the inhabitants of these concealed dimensions are called demons and are set against humanity. They have the very intentional agenda of destroying humans. Sadly, they influence everyone who is not under God's protection.

The apostle Paul, one of the most spiritually intelligent people ever to grace this earth, wrote, "You were dead in your trespasses and sins, in which you formerly walked *according to the course of this world, according to the prince of the power of the air, of the spirit that is now working in the sons of disobedience*" (Ephesians 2:1–2, emphasis added). I know this may sound like science fiction to you, but it is real.

The good news is that there are more angels who are for us than there are demons who are against us. God has assigned strong angelic allies to help us in life and in battle. The ability to *distinguish* or *discern* these spiritual entities and their *angelic* (those who are for us) or *demonic* (those who are against us) strategies is essential to the true success of every person on the planet. It is also important to understand that believers have been given gifts and authority over this unseen realm, to undermine and disarm the devious demonic agendas.

The Gift of Spiritual Eyes and Ears

The gift of discernment is mentioned in 1 Corinthians 12:10 and is demonstrated in Acts 16. This gift is to the spirit realm what a radio is to the natural realm. A radio takes radio waves, which are undetectable to our natural senses, and converts them into sound waves that we can hear and decode. In the same way, the gift of discernment takes the invisible world and converts it into something detectable. This gift of the Spirit, among other spiritual gifts, acts as our divine eyes and ears. Let's take a look at how the apostle Paul's gift of discernment assisted him in his encounter with a demonized girl:

It happened that as we were going to the place of prayer, a slave-girl having a spirit of divination met us, who was bringing her masters much profit by fortune-telling. Following after Paul and us, she kept crying out, saying, "These men are bond-servants of the Most High God, who are proclaiming to you the way of salvation." She continued doing this for many days. But Paul was greatly annoyed, and turned and said to the spirit, "I command you in the name of Jesus Christ to come out of her!" And it came out at that very moment.

Acts 16:16–18

We should understand some important things from this story. Our first insight is that even though the slave girl was telling the truth, Paul discerned that the *spiritual source* of her insights was rooted in the demonic realm, not in the Holy Spirit. When Paul commanded the spirit of divination to leave her, she could no longer tell the future. Then her bosses got so mad about her inability to foretell the future that they had Paul and his friend arrested.

A second powerful observation I want to make is that like the Midway attack plot to lure the American ships into a destructive trap through deception and deceit, Satan also uses deceptive and deceitful people to entice us into devastating situations. As we see here, he sometimes even uses demonic spirits to inspire people under his influence to give *positive information* to people to win a place of influence with them. But his ultimate goal is *always bad*. I repeat, it is *always bad*!

Psychics in the Church

Like the apostle Paul, our team has had several experiences with psychics over the years. One of the most memorable encounters happened after an evening meeting at a church on the coast, when roughly thirty of us were ministering to a few hundred people who had stayed after the teaching time for prayer. We removed the chairs and organized the waiting people into rows in the sanctuary. For a couple of hours, we spent time ministering to each person individually.

In the midst of the evening, we met a lady dressed in a nice business suit. She surprised us when we asked how we could pray for her, answering, "I'm a psychic, and I have worked as one for several large companies over the last decade. But I've been tormented for a long time now, and I don't know what to do about it. I have a friend who *was* also a psychic and *was* really tormented. He came to a service a while back, and you guys prayed for him. Now he's living in complete peace. He told me to ask for you."

Frankly, we were surprised by her honesty, humility and transparency. While she was talking, the Holy Spirit showed us the problem, so I responded, "Here's the issue: You have two spirit guides giving you insights into the future. Is this true?"

"Yes!" she said excitedly.

"Well, the problem is that your spirit guides are actually demons. They are the ones tormenting you." I was trying to be gentle because I knew she thought these guides were her friends.

She looked confused. "You mean that my spirit guides are actually dark spirits, like evil entities?"

"Yep," I said matter-of-factly. "If I make them leave, you'll have your peace back," I continued.

"Okay," she said, obviously trying to think through the ramifications of ditching her two "friends." "If I don't have my spirit guides, will I be able to tell the future?"

"No," I said. I knew the Lord could, and likely would, give her spiritual intelligence that would be far more profound than the demons she was listening to. Nevertheless, I felt as though I was to tell her no.

"So if I can't tell the future, how will I make a living?" she inquired.

"I'm not sure. But let me put it like this: You can be wealthy and tormented, or you can be broke and peaceful. Those are your two options," I explained. I knew there were other possibilities, but the

Spirit told me she was like the rich young ruler, and she needed to leave everything to follow Jesus.

"Let me think about it," she replied in a contemplative tone. I started to walk away, thinking she would go home and count the cost. Instead, she bowed her head and closed her eyes for a couple of minutes. Then she looked up and said, "I'd rather have peace like my friend has!"

I was honestly a little surprised. "Okay, let's do this!" I said. "Now, if we make these spirit guides leave, you'll need to ask Jesus into your life and follow Him. The Holy Spirit will be your Spirit Guide," I explained. "Otherwise, those evil spirits will forcibly return and really mess up your life."

"Yes, my friend told me he asked Jesus into his life. He explained that he's now being led by the Spirit of Jesus," she responded.

I put my hand on her head, with her permission, and began to pray. She looked up and said, "My spirit guides said to tell you they don't like you!"

I pushed back, "Tell them I don't like them either!"

"They said to tell you they know you hate them," she said.

A few minutes later, we commanded her spirit guides to leave her. Suddenly, she fell on the floor and shook under the power of the Holy Spirit. She lay there for an hour, and then finally got up off the floor and thanked Jesus for her freedom. It was exhilarating to watch the countenance of someone who was tormented by demons change at being filled with the Spirit!

Discerning Evil Spirits

You might be hearing these stories and think that you could never do this kind of stuff. Actually, if you are a follower of Jesus, you are called to have these kinds of encounters. I wrote an entire book titled *Spirit Wars* that outlines my personal journey into this subject. In fact, as I was writing this SQ book, I often found myself wanting to share with you something I had already written in *Spirit Wars*, because spiritual warfare is such a crucial part of SQ. So let me introduce you more deeply to the "decoding" side of spiritual intelligence by exposing you to a few paragraphs from chapter 11 of *Spirit Wars*, which I called "On-the-Job Training."

The gift of discernment operates differently through various people. The most common way this gift manifests in us is that we feel, hear, smell or taste whatever spirit is troubling the person whose metron we are in.

Before we get deeper into the subject of discernment, we need to refresh our memories about metrons and the spheres of authority. . . . This concept comes from the meaning of two Greek words. The first is *metron*, meaning "measure" or "standard." The second is *kanon*, meaning "to rule a sphere." Both words are used in Paul's exhortation to the Corinthians. Read it slowly:

We will not boast beyond our *measure* [Greek root word *metron*], but within the *measure* [*metron*] of the *sphere* [Greek word *kanon*] which God apportioned to us as a *measure* [*metron*], to reach even as far as you . . . not boasting beyond our *measure* [*metron*], that is, in other men's labors, but with the hope that as your faith grows, we will be, within our *sphere* [*kanon*], enlarged even more by you.

2 Corinthians 10:13, 15, emphasis added

Simply stated, Paul is saying that the people of Corinth are within the boundaries of his God-given spiritual authority. . . . Every person has a metron (measured space) that he or she rules over or influences. The size of people's metrons is determined by their God-given spiritual influence. A metron can be restricted to the size of an individual, or it can be as large as his or her sphere of authority.

For example, have you ever walked into a store and immediately felt exhausted? You quickly purchased the things you needed and left. As soon as you got into your vehicle and drove away, you were fine . . . the tired feeling had lifted. Most likely, the manager or owner of that store had a spirit of fatigue or fainting. (Isaiah 61:3 says that the Lord will give us "the mantle of praise instead of a spirit of fainting.") Because *all* authority is from God and it is He who determines the size of a person's metron (see Romans 13:1; 2 Corinthians 10:13–15), an owner's or manager's metron would be the size of the store. When you walked into the store, you actually were entering the spiritual space of the person in authority there, and you were discerning the ruling spirits the person had invited into that "space."

On a personal level, if you have the gift of discernment and you sit next to someone troubled by an evil spirit of pornography, you most likely will experience pornographic thoughts or pictures while you are in that person's "space." Or if you touch someone dealing with a demon of depression, you suddenly will feel depressed. I should make it clear that the spirit realm affects all Christians, whether they are aware of it or not. The gift of discernment simply gives you the ability to distinguish what spirit or spirits are at work in a person or an environment.

Counseling Tools

When I first joined the staff at Bethel Church, one of my main responsibilities was counseling. When people would come into my office for counsel, I would lay hands on them and pray before I let them tell me why they came to see me. I would pray for wisdom and insight, but honestly, what I was really doing was touching them so that I could discern if an evil spirit was involved in their situation. If I laid hands on a person and I was not troubled by something, then I knew whatever the counselee was dealing with was purely human and not demonic. On the other hand, if I felt rage, murder, hatred, fear, paranoia or any other negative manifestation, I knew that evil spirits had attached themselves to the situation and therefore counseling alone would not solve the person's issue. We would have to make sure that we expelled the evil spirits after we dealt with the root causes of their invitation. . . .

While we are talking about discernment, I also want to warn you about suspicion. Suspicion is discernment's wicked stepsister. It can masquerade as discernment and ultimately lead us into bondage. Suspicion is the gift of discernment being used by the spirit of fear. For example, before King Saul was tormented by demons, the Bible says that "Saul looked at David with suspicion from that day on" (1 Samuel 18:9). Suspicion leads to bitterness, unforgiveness and torment; it will result in a person being cast into a spiritual prison where all the guards work for the dark side. The spirits who guard the bars of this prison have names like sickness, depression, hatred and murder. . . .

When you have a strong negative opinion about someone, do not trust your "gift of discernment." Solomon said that a good name is more desirable than great wealth (see Proverbs 22:1). The goal of any gift of the Spirit is to build trust and help people grow in God. No gift of the Spirit should be used to destroy people's reputations, kill their passion for God or steal their identity. Even if your discernment proves accurate and a demonic spirit is troubling a person, that person's reputation should be protected and his or her personhood should always be honored as someone created in the likeness of God.*

Entering Uncharted Waters

There is so much to learn and uncover about the spirit world. Most of this realm is uncharted water. The fact that Satan masquerades as an angel of light, or as a wolf in sheep's clothing, adds an element of treachery to our spiritual journey. His devious schemes are seldom obvious since he is crazy but not stupid.

Discerning the source of our own and others' spiritual encounters is therefore paramount to leading a healthy life in God and becoming a truly spiritually intelligent person. Unfortunately, many well-meaning believers are gullible and/or even downright naïve to the wiles of this unseen yet powerful realm. Some have even become victims of the devil's devices.

* Kris Vallotton, *Spirit Wars: Winning the Invisible Battle against Sin and the Enemy* (Minneapolis: Chosen, 2012), 172–176.

But the good news is that God has provided us with all the tools we need to navigate the spirit realm with wisdom and grace, knowing that the Holy Spirit is our tour guide, our divine conductor and our loving protector. Living our lives rooted in Him is therefore an exuberant adventure—an exploration into the very depths of God.

9

The Demise of Spiritual Intelligence

Real spiritual intelligence transcends memory, is beyond mere information and exceeds academia. That's right—spiritual intelligence is more than inspired ideas, creative thoughts or ingenious inventions, although it certainly includes these dimensions (as I've already illustrated). Spiritual intelligence is not just *knowing*. It is *becoming*, it is *transforming*, and it is a *force for change* that is working on us from the inside out.

This life-changing side of spiritual intelligence is always catalyzed through relationships between God and His people. In a relational transfer of information, a dynamic takes place in which the recipient experiences transformation in his inner man (or her inner person, to include the ladies). Literally, information comes alive in the context of specific kinds of relationships. Let me illustrate this with these words of Jesus: "A pupil is not above his teacher; but everyone, after he has been fully trained, will be like his teacher" (Luke 6:40).

In other words, when information is delivered through the context of discipleship, we are not just learning; we are becoming like the

One who teaches us—in this case Jesus. The Parable of the Sower emphasizes this, in which Jesus taught us that the Kingdom is planted in the lives of people, just as a sower plants seeds in his field. The three main elements in this parable are the sower, who is God; the seed, which is the Kingdom; and the soil, which represents our hearts. Check out Matthew 13:20–21:

> The one on whom seed was sown on the rocky places, this is the man who hears the word and immediately receives it with joy; yet he has no firm root in himself, but is only temporary, and when affliction or persecution arises because of the word, immediately he falls away.

The Greek word here for *seed* is the word *sperma*, which means "offspring." We get our English word *sperm* from this word. Notice how the seed that falls on rocky soil is described as falling on a man who has "no firm root in himself."

It may seem odd that someone has to prepare to receive the Kingdom, until you realize that the Kingdom is being transferred in the form of a seed or sperm. It makes sense that something coming from another world needs to be protected from the hostile elements of this world. This revelation was instilled in me in 2006, when Kathy and I went to Hawaii for the first time. As we began to drive our rental car down the highway in Maui, Kathy shouted, "Stop! Pull over!"

"What's wrong?" I asked.

"Do you see that huge tree on the side of the road? That's the small plant we have in our bathroom!"

"Great," I responded, trying to get my heart to stop pounding out of my chest.

We drove on a little farther. "Look over there!" Kathy said excitedly, pointing to another very large plant. "There's the little plant we have on our kitchen sink."

"Wonderful," I conceded. This scene was repeated throughout our entire visit to the island. It finally occurred to me that there is no such thing as an indoor plant. There are only plants created to live in another environment. When we take them out of their natural habitat, we have to create an artificial environment for them so that they will survive the elements.

In the same way, the seed of God was created to live in another Kingdom. This world is a hostile environment to the life of God. The embryo of His Word needs a womb—an artificial environment that protects it from this world's elements, until that seed grows into life within us. The apostle Paul put it like this: "My children, with whom I am again in labor until Christ is formed in you" (Galatians 4:19). Paul labored among them through teaching and preaching. He was a sower, sowing the seed of the Kingdom into the "wombs" of his people.

So the million-dollar question is, *How* do we "receive the word implanted, which is able to save your souls" (James 1:21)? A womb for that seed is formed in us through instruction. The word *instruction* actually means "structures formed in me." In other words, instruction fashions a sort of womb within us so that we can receive "teaching," which in the context of this kind of spiritual intelligence is "information," or more accurately, "the Kingdom forming within us."

I used to think that teaching and instruction were the same things, but I was wrong. The Hebrew word *musar* and the Greek word *paideia* are most often translated "instruction" in our English Bible. They mean "discipline, chastening, correction, punishment, reproof and warning." The implication is that instruction is education or training through disciplinary action. That's why we are called disciples. The word *disciple* means "learner," but it comes from the word *discipline*. This dynamic is demonstrated in the book of Proverbs, in which Solomon, describing a foolish person, writes, "How I have hated instruction! And my heart spurned reproof!" (Proverbs 5:12). Notice in this passage how instruction is a manifestation of reproof.

On the other hand, the Hebrew word *leqach* and the Greek word *didasko* are most often translated "to teach" or "teaching" in our

English Bible. They mean "to persuade, learn or receive." Teaching is literally the process of receiving revelation, and it is the gathering of information.

Now let's go back to the story of the sower. Jesus said the man had no root in himself, so the seed died. Roots are formed through the ability to receive instruction, or "structures within." If we refuse correction, reproof, discipline and chastening, we will not have a womb to protect the seeds of teaching. Teaching comes from receiving information, or internal formations. Remember, the goal of developing this type of SQ is that Christ is actually being formed within us. In other words, we are "becoming" the teaching, just as Jesus demonstrated when the Bible says of Him that "the Word became flesh, and dwelt among us" (John 1:14).

My Experience

Over the years, I have discipled many people. I have grieved numerous times over people whom I have poured my life into, only to have them later fall away from Jesus.

As a matter of fact, a few of the leaders I spent the most time with in my earlier years of ministry no longer walk with God today. I performed most of their weddings and was around when their children were born. Frankly, I have wept long hours over them and wondered what I did wrong in leading them. I wondered if I could have done a better job discipling them.

But looking back, I remember one thing that troubled me about all of them: None of them could ever take correction. They always seemed to have an excuse about why things were not their fault. Now they have become walking dead men and women whom I will love forever.

I have learned through these experiences that we must embrace the discipline of God that comes through human agency, as it cultivates the culture of the Kingdom within us.

The Plight of Solomon

One of the saddest stories in the Bible is a tale of the ultimate demise of King Solomon, the wisest man in the world. God gave him supernatural wisdom that was so profound that kings and queens traveled for months just to experience his insights. Much of his extreme wealth was the result of these kings and queens honoring him with their treasures.

In those precious years, Solomon penned the book of Proverbs, which is to this day the most profound display of wisdom sayings ever assembled into one book. His insights are timeless, his understanding is profound, and his instruction is transforming. But in his later years, Solomon exchanged his relationship with God for foreign women. In the midst of his disconnection with God, he wrote the book of Ecclesiastes.

While it is true that "the gifts and the calling of God are irrevocable" (Romans 11:29), the book of Ecclesiastes shows us what happens when the wisest man in the world loses connection with his God. Solomon's wisdom became a mixture of wise and foolish contemplations. His soul was deeply vexed with a terrible sense of meaninglessness, which was displayed in his constant use of the words *vanity* and *futility*.

The perplexing thing about the life of Solomon is that he warned us all about the very kinds of things he ended up practicing, and ultimately, he became the most famous hypocrite in the Bible.

Wisdom

I want to take you through just a few of the many conflicting ideas of Solomon that highlight the danger of cultivating spiritual intelligence absent of a relationship with God. To me, this also highlights the challenge of helping people who don't walk with God tap into the gift without knowing the Giver. It is a sobering lesson that I have observed playing out too many times in the lives of those around me.

As a humble king in a close relationship with God, here are some of Solomon's exhortations in Proverbs on the pursuit of wisdom:

> How blessed is the man who finds wisdom and the man who gains understanding. For her profit is better than the profit of silver and her gain better than fine gold. She is more precious than jewels; and nothing you desire compares with her. Long life is in her right hand; in her left hand are riches and honor. Her ways are pleasant ways and all her paths are peace. She is a tree of life to those who take hold of her, and happy are all who hold her fast. The LORD by wisdom founded the earth, by understanding He established the heavens.
>
> Proverbs 3:13–19

> Acquire wisdom! Acquire understanding! Do not forget nor turn away from the words of my mouth. Do not forsake her, and she will guard you; love her, and she will watch over you.
>
> Proverbs 4:5–6

Now, here is one of Solomon's musings on the same subject of wisdom in his later years, when he was disconnected from God and became steeped in the philosophies of foreign gods:

> I saw that wisdom excels folly as light excels darkness. The wise man's eyes are in his head, but the fool walks in darkness. And yet I know that one fate befalls them both. Then I said to myself, "As is the fate of the fool, it will also befall me. Why then have I been extremely wise?" So I said to myself, "This too is vanity."
>
> Ecclesiastes 2:13–15

The word *vanity* that Solomon uses throughout the book of Ecclesiastes is the Hebrew word *hebel*, meaning "delusion, empty, fleeting, fraud, futility, useless and worthless." In other words, in

Proverbs Solomon taught us to get wisdom at any price. He went on to say that wisdom is the most prized possession of God. But in Ecclesiastes, he tells us that becoming wise is useless and worthless. In fact, he states that the same fate befalls the wise man and the fool. In case you are wondering, neither of Solomon's statements in Ecclesiastes is true!

Inheritance

Here is another of Solomon's great insights in Proverbs, this time on the subject of inheritance:

> A good man leaves an inheritance to his children's children, and the wealth of the sinner is stored up for the righteous.

> Proverbs 13:22

Now read Solomon's coldhearted exhortation in Ecclesiastes on leaving a legacy to his children:

> When there is a man who has labored with wisdom, knowledge and skill, then he gives his legacy to one who has not labored with them. This too is vanity and a great evil. For what does a man get in all his labor and in his striving with which he labors under the sun? Because all his days his task is painful and grievous; even at night his mind does not rest. This too is vanity.

> Ecclesiastes 2:21–23

Again, Solomon contradicts his own book of Proverbs with his later book and concludes that leaving a legacy is meaningless and worthless.

It is important to note here that Solomon's son, Rehoboam, became king after him. Rehoboam's mother, Naamah, was one of the foreign wives Solomon married and was an Ammonitess. King Rehoboam inherited his father's wealth, but his kingship was steeped in Ecclesiastes, not Proverbs. Sadly, the glory days of King David and King Solomon (in his early years) were lost for centuries in King Rehoboam and beyond.

Righteousness

One of the most disturbing contrasts between Solomon's two books is on the subject of righteousness. Here are a couple of verses on the subject from Proverbs, although there are many more:

> The name of the LORD is a strong tower; the righteous runs into it and is safe.
>
> Proverbs 18:10

> The heart of the righteous ponders how to answer, but the mouth of the wicked pours out evil things. The LORD is far from the wicked, but He hears the prayer of the righteous.
>
> Proverbs 15:28–29

Now, here are thoughts on the same subject from a foolish king with the gift of wisdom:

> Do not be excessively righteous and do not be overly wise. Why should you ruin yourself? Do not be excessively wicked and do not be a fool. Why should you die before your time?
>
> Ecclesiastes 7:16–17

Really? Being too righteous will ruin you? Actually, what ruined Solomon was his lack of righteousness, which ultimately led him into deception and destroyed his legacy.

Money

The last subject we will investigate concerns money. Being the richest man in the history of the world should have given Solomon some insights into the subject of wealth, and here is one from Proverbs:

Do not weary yourself to gain wealth, cease from your consideration of it. When you set your eyes on it, it is gone. For wealth certainly makes itself wings like an eagle that flies toward the heavens.

Proverbs 23:4–5

But when this king lost connection with the Lord, he had this to say about wealth instead:

Men prepare a meal for enjoyment, and wine makes life merry, and money is the answer to everything.

Ecclesiastes 10:19

Money is the answer to everything?! Solomon, this is your profound insight into the secret of life—get rich? No!

The pressing question all these contradictions raise is why the book of Ecclesiastes is even in the Bible. In my mind, there are two reasons. First, there is some profound wisdom scattered throughout the book's verses. A verse's wisdom is often undone, however, in the very next verse because Solomon was so deceived.

Yet remember, as I stated earlier, that the gifts and the calling of God are irrevocable. This means that when God gives a person a gift, He never takes it back. So second, although some of Ecclesiastes is actually true and even profoundly revelatory, ultimately the overarching message of that book demonstrates what happens when the wisest man on earth loses his relationship with his God.

The Goal

I hope it is clear by now that true spiritual intelligence is more than just being smart; it is about being wise, noble, influenceable and correctable. There are a lot of smart people in the world, even some with photographic memories and multiple Ph.D.s, who have the wisdom of Ecclesiastes.

Other people are geniuses on a certain subject, but they can hardly navigate normal, everyday life. It is alarming to watch smart people who have no wisdom make destructive choices for themselves and for those they influence. Or just as troubling is watching someone who once loved God and walked in His wisdom, filled with His goodness, exchanging it all for empty, immediate gratification.

I want this book to inspire everyone who reads it to receive the mind of Christ and experience spiritual intelligence on a level that has never occurred in the history of the world. Yet I am aware that the most spiritually intelligent thing we can do is love God and love people—not passively, but passionately, pursuing our connections with courage and humility. It is important that we never forget that we are His disciples!

10

The Science of SQ

The apostle Paul had a stunning revelation concerning the nature of God. He wrote, "For since the creation of the world His invisible attributes, His eternal power and divine nature, have been clearly seen, being understood through what has been made, so that they are without excuse" (Romans 1:20). In other words, the attributes, power and nature of the Creator are revealed through His creation. Science is not anti-God; it is pro-revelation.

Think about it like this: There is an idiom that says, "If only these walls could talk," which is usually applied to the secret conversations of very important and/or influential people. Yet in the truest sense, God's walls do talk! In fact, everything God made has a voice that begs to whisper the secret mysteries of the Master. These next verses are stunning:

The heavens declare the glory of God; the skies proclaim the work of his hands. Day after day they pour forth speech; night after night they reveal knowledge. They have no speech, they use no words; no sound is heard from them. Yet their voice goes out into all the earth, their words to the ends of the world. In the heavens God has pitched a tent for the sun. It is like a bridegroom coming out of his chamber, like a champion rejoicing to run his course. It rises at one end of the heavens and makes its circuit to the other; nothing is deprived of its warmth.

Psalm 19:1–6 NIV

Notice that creation is shouting revelation about God's nature in deafening silence. In a scientific sense, God buried time capsules in every cell of creation. Paul went on to say in Romans 1 that unbelief is inexcusable because creation makes an ironclad case for God. Creation is actually proclaiming the Gospel, and real science is God's personal assistant. It's hard to think of the glory of creation without being inspired to think *bigger*. Then add the Lord's Prayer to creation's glory, and suddenly you begin to reach for the stars and actually believe that it could be "on earth as it is in heaven."

Additionally, a few thousand years ago the prophet Habakkuk declared, "The earth will be filled with the knowledge of the glory of the LORD, as the waters cover the sea" (Habakkuk 2:14). The question is, *When?* When will the "knowledge of the glory of the Lord" be as deep as the ocean and as broad as the sea? Why not here, and why not now? Daniel prophesied that in the last days, knowledge would increase. I have heard people say that the Internet and the Information Age are the fulfillment of Daniel's vision. I disagree! I don't think the Internet is the fulfillment of the prophecy; I think it is the vehicle, the vessel and the receptacle necessary to carry out Habakkuk's vision.

Initiate the Plan

With this in mind, and after years of intense and persistent pressing against the religious mindsets that inhibit real progress, the Bethel Leadership Team decided to get out of the boat and actually do something wild. So in January 2018, we hired Ryan Collins as our

CEO and started Bethel School of Technology, the first faith-based coding school in the world. We call it "Coding with a Cause." Here is a short overview of its mission and vision that I hope inspires you!

Bethel School of Technology is a faith-based, values-driven online technology bootcamp that specializes in the high-demand areas of Software Development, Data Science, and UI/UX Design. Our school exists to raise up ready-to-work Christian technologists who serve companies with excellence in both skill and character.

Starting with "Coding from Scratch," our nine-month program is designed to help individuals with little or no tech background learn the necessary skills to upstart an in-demand, high-growth career in the tech space. Students receive focused support from instructors, who have extensive experience in the tech industry, and weekly code reviews with coding mentors. Additionally, seasoned developers and executives from some of the leading tech companies, including Google, IBM and Facebook, volunteer their time to host workshops on what it takes to break into the tech industry and exhibit high EQ in the workplace.*

Here is some exciting news: In 2020, just eighteen months after we launched Bethel Tech, *Newsweek* rated it as one of the top five technology bootcamps in America. "Why start a coding camp?" you ask. Because we have a deep desire to change the world, and we understand that if we want to affect the world in the Information Age, then we must gain influence in the "information gates." Much like Daniel in Babylon, who was required to learn the literature and language of the Chaldeans before he and his three friends could serve in the king's court, we must raise up modern-day Daniels who can serve the kings of the earth. It is imperative that these modern Daniels also know "the language of the Chaldeans," so to speak. In fact, this coincides with the ultimate purpose of this book: to

---

* *Newsweek* Educational Insight, *Newsweek* online, "The Top Coding School of 2019: Sponsor Insight Bethel School of Technology," https://www.newsweek.com/insights/the-top -coding-schools-of-2019/bethel-school-technology.

discover, develop and deploy the Daniels and Esthers of the Kingdom to serve the kings of the earth not only with IQ and EQ, but with SQ—spiritual intelligence.

There is a great story in the book of Judges that depicts a sudden shift of authority in the enemy's gates (authority is often depicted metaphorically as gates in the Bible). Part of it reads, "Samson . . . arose and took hold of the doors of the city gate and the two posts and pulled them up along with the bars; then he put them on his shoulders and carried them up to the top of the mountain" (Judges 16:3). I realize that Samson's exploit is not a fairy tale; it's actually a true story of a man endowed with the supernatural power to displace the gates of the enemy. But I also see the story as a twenty-first-century prophetic mandate from God to unearth the information gates and carry them to the mountain of the Lord, the high places of God, where the knowledge of the glory of the Lord begins to dictate the mindsets of the multitudes.

Ryan's Perspective

Ryan Collins, CEO of Bethel Tech, is a young man in his late thirties who has a decade of experience in the bootcamp tech space. Before he came to Bethel, he helped build one of the largest bootcamps in the world. In those days, he thought science and technology were relegated to the world. Here is Ryan's spiritual journey in his own words:

> When we started Bethel School of Technology, I held the assumption that the tech space was a direct result of humanism. Other major sectors, like education and healthcare, began with overt Christian foundations. But in tech, it has always been widely understood that innovation comes from human critical thinking, alone. Over the last year, however, God has been shifting my perspective on this assumption, opening my eyes to the genesis of our modern communication networks that drive the tech space—Wi-Fi, television, mobile phones,

etc. I couldn't shake the notion that the natures of these innovations all have one thing in common: They are dependent upon an underlying reality to function through unseen frequencies. Further, I couldn't overlook the parallels between the manifestation of a hidden realm in the natural world and how it mirrored our multidimensional relationship with God, which is noted in 1 Corinthians 2:9–10 and 16:

> But as it is written: Eye has not seen, nor ear heard, nor have entered into the heart of man the things which God has prepared for those who love Him. But God has revealed them to us through His spirit. . . . For "who has known the mind of the LORD that he may instruct Him?" But we have the mind of Christ.

So, how did humanity get to the point that we could operate in an unseen realm if we didn't know that it first existed? Unless, of course, a precedent was set in modern science in which humans thought and functioned in a hidden realm to pull unseen ideas and solutions into our natural world.

This curiosity led me to explore the life and discoveries of the Scottish physicist James Clerk Maxwell, who lived in the mid- to late 1800s. Maxwell is considered the greatest scientist between Isaac Newton and Albert Einstein. In fact, when Einstein was asked, "Do you stand on the shoulders of Newton?" he simply responded, "No, I stand on the shoulders of Maxwell."

It was Maxwell who ushered in a revolution in the way scientists viewed the natural world. He dared to look at objects and forces in the physical realm as one part of a larger equation, and he believed there had to be an underlying reality, inaccessible by our senses, that could be described mathematically. It was this underlying reality or "undreamt-of region," as he called it, which provided further insight into how objects and forces in the physical realm operated and existed.

From this posture, Maxwell discovered that light itself was an electromagnetic wave. And, through manipulation of these waves, the information could be transferred from one place to the next through empty space. Hence, no space is actually empty. Our great communication networks of today—radio, television, satellite, mobile phones and Wi-Fi, are all the fruit of Maxwell's theories and discoveries.

Furthermore, Maxwell was a radical Christian! He believed God and science were not mutually exclusive, but eternally linked—that God the Creator made us in His own image and gave us dominion over His creation. Maxwell also believed it was our privilege and responsibility to study the works of our Creator. As he stated, "Let nothing be left willfully unexamined." The more we leaned in and explored the work of our Creator's hands, Maxwell was convinced, the more God would reveal His creation to us, through us and with us, pulling the unseen into the seen. Our modern world was built on the shoulders of Maxwell's spiritual intelligence.

Today, I believe we are on the verge of the next epoch season of technological innovation, and it will be ushered in largely by quantum computing (for which Maxwell is recognized as paving the way nearly 150 years ago). At its premise, quantum computing points to a multidimensional nature in which physical objects are permanently connected in an underlying reality. With quantum computing, the idea is that there is an exponentially faster, more optimized way to store, transport and compute data than classical computing. Whereas a classical computer uses bits to represent the values it is operating on, a quantum computer uses *qubits*. A bit can either be 0 or 1, while a qubit can represent the values 0 or 1, or some combination of both at the same time, known as superposition.

To be clear, I'm not a quantum physicist, and my understanding of the concept is at a fifty-thousand-foot view. But I find the theory fascinating and worth exploring to tell a larger story, particularly in the aforementioned "superposition" and "entanglement."

In superposition, a qubit holds two binary values at once. This is achieved by spinning the qubit—similar to spinning a coin, in which during the spin, the coin is both heads and tails. When two separate qubits are in superposition, they can be linked together with quantum entanglement.

In entanglement, two separate and apart qubits become exactly correlated, so that whatever one is, the other is also. They become mirror images of each other. Information is transported instantaneously from one qubit to another because the transport is not a matter of transferring through time and space; rather, it's a matter of being what the other is. Einstein called this quantum mechanics "spooky action at a distance." Imagine how fast we could access data in a quantum computer compared to a classical computer. There is no dimension of time and space to distort the communication.

Quantum computing represents a more perfect (albeit complex) method of sending and receiving data than classical computing. Experts believe that we are anywhere from five years to decades away from quantum computing becoming mainstream. Last month, scientists at the University of Bristol and the Technical University of Denmark achieved quantum teleportation between two computer chips (called qubits) for the first time.

The chief tech companies in the world are now in a race to re-imagine the computer using quantum mechanics, and they are employing the leading quantum physicists, who are splitting the atom into smaller subatomic particles. What they are finding when they further dissect the atom into smaller particles is that these particles move and function in an inexplicable way—to the point that many scientists have determined that there must be a guiding force in another universe directing the movements of the particles.

A friend of mine who works in R&D at one of the leading tech companies explained it to me this way: "The closer we look at physics and particles, the more we realize we don't really understand what 'matter' even is, and the only way we can accurately model or represent particle physics is by assuming infinitive worlds or alternative realities actually exist. The deeper we go in quantum science, the stranger and more bizarre the theories must become in order to explain their reality."

What I find interesting about where science and tech innovation is headed is that it appears to be pointing toward an advanced state of operating in both the natural world and heavenly realm simultaneously. Think about it: In superposition, a qubit when spun can be in two states simultaneously—much like humans, who are here on earth, but also are simultaneously seated in heavenly places.

In entanglement, two objects become mirror images of each other. A measurement of one will immediately determine the measurement of the other, regardless of distance. Information can be transferred instantly because it is not being transported through space. What one object is, the other is also, simultaneously. There is no transferring of knowledge. As children of God, we have the mind of Christ. We don't just know of God; we know Him and are "entangled" as one with Him.

This is a beautiful picture of the way God has communion with His children, while also actualizing the revelation of Immanuel, Christ with us, and Christ through us. Subsequently, we pull solutions from the unseen realm into our natural world to help people—solutions that will serve as building blocks to expand His Kingdom.

Maxwell stated, "Every atom of creation is unfathomable in its perfection." There will come a point in the history of science where we explore creation so deeply that the inevitable and irrefutable truth of the Creator is revealed. Consequently, science is actually unveiling the mysteries of heaven on Earth, and Christ with us, even at the hands of individuals who have yet to see themselves as children of God. They are building upon Maxwell's spiritual intelligence, and they don't even know it!

It is important to recognize that our modern world was founded on the principle of partnering with the Holy Spirit to pull ideas from the hidden realm to the natural. And yet, the Church isn't typically associated with this type of innovation, even though we have the mind of Christ and are called to have His manifold wisdom. What if we unlock the next epoch season in innovation and it is accelerated by the next Maxwell (or better yet, Maxwells), who use spiritual intelligence to pull innovations from the "undreamt-of" region into our physical world? What if these innovations are fully actualized by using them the way that God designed them, to help people have an encounter with Christ? I propose that we would see a revival to and through the tech space in which all would see and encounter the goodness of God and know Him as Lord.

Reflecting on his life, right before his death, Maxwell said, "The only desire which I can have is, like David, to serve my own generation by the will of God, and then fall asleep." Our modern world was built on the shoulders of Maxwell, a believer who used spiritual intelligence to discover that information could be transferred through empty space, and who created a foundation for what eventually became the tech space.

We've Only Just Begun

Ryan is a modern-day pioneer who is venturing deep into the unseen world of quantum mechanics by proactively tapping into spiritual intelligence. He will one day be known as one of the forerunners of our time. Yet, about 1,800 years before Maxwell and 1,950 years before Ryan Collins, around AD 70 the writer of Hebrews said, "By faith we understand that the worlds were prepared by the word of God, so that what is seen was not made out of things which are visible" (Hebrews 11:3). Of course, like most people, I thought that the Hebrew author was merely pointing out that the spirit realm was initiated first, followed by the natural dimension. This is altogether possible, but the verse doesn't say anything about "spiritual" and "natural." It actually says that the visible came from the invisible. It is intriguing to think that faith may be the key to science and that SQ may unlock the door to the mysteries of creation.

The apostle Paul wrote one of the most captivating concepts in the entire Bible in Ephesians 3:8–10. We looked at these verses earlier, but let's read them slowly this time and let them sink into our spirit:

> To me, the very least of all saints, this grace was given, to preach to the Gentiles the unfathomable riches of Christ, and to bring to light what is the administration of the mystery which for ages has been hidden in God who created all things; so that the manifold wisdom of God might now be made known through the church to the rulers and the authorities in the heavenly places.

The Greek word *manifold* here means "multicolored" or "having many dimensions." It is therefore clear that God wants the Church to teach the mysteries of the ages to rulers and authorities in the heavenly places. Some may limit this revelation to understanding the salvation of the Gentiles or that Christ in us is the hope of glory. But it seems to me that there is a revelation of creation just waiting to be discovered that will unlock the very nature of God Himself! The apostle Paul also wrote this epic revelation about Jesus:

> He is the exact likeness of the unseen God [the visible representation of the invisible]; He is the Firstborn of all creation.
>
> For it was in Him that all things were created, in heaven and on earth, things seen and things unseen, whether thrones, dominions, rulers, or authorities; all things were created and exist through Him [by His service, intervention] and in and for Him.
>
> And He Himself existed before all things, and in Him all things consist (cohere, are held together).
>
> Colossians 1:15–17 AMPC

Christ holds everything in the visible and invisible world together cohesively. In other words, Christ Himself controls the invisible force that causes visible matter to (seemingly) magically form or intrinsically connect at the molecular level.

If you think about it, it makes perfect sense, as God is not "in heaven"; heaven is in God. Solomon said, "Behold, heaven and the highest heaven cannot contain You" (1 Kings 8:27). Jesus said, "Heaven and earth will pass away, but My words will not pass away" (Mark 13:31). Heaven and earth are finite, but His Word is infinite. If heaven is not eternal, but is a created realm or place, then where did God live before there was heaven? It should be obvious that God has to be bigger than heaven, since He is eternal and heaven is finite. There is therefore no way heaven can contain God. So from a finite perspective God is our heavenly Father, as we were instructed to pray *Our Father who is in heaven* in the Lord's Prayer—

with an understanding that we also (hopefully) have an earthly father.

Yet the Bible is clear from an infinite perspective, further declaring that "the heavens and the highest heavens cannot contain Him" (2 Chronicles 2:6). Isaiah went on to prophesy, "Thus says the LORD, 'Heaven is My throne and the earth is My footstool'" (Isaiah 66:1). When you understand creation from an eternal perspective, then Isaiah's prophecy takes on an entirely different perspective. Heaven and earth are God's furniture; they facilitate Him, but they don't confine Him!

Now let's go back to my main point, that Jesus is the creator and source of all matter, and that He holds it all together. He is the source of the invisible yet tangible magnetic force—the electromagnetic energy—that glues matter together at the very core of its atomic structure. It's not by chance that the first thing God ever spoke into existence was light:

> In the beginning God created the heavens and the earth. The earth was formless and void, and darkness was over the surface of the deep, and the Spirit of God was moving over the surface of the waters. Then God said, "Let there be light"; and there was light.
>
> Genesis 1:1–3

The earth was *formless* and *void*. The word *formless* is the Hebrew word *tohu*, meaning "confusion, chaos, desolation or a waste place." The Hebrew word for *void* is *bohu*, meaning "emptiness." God's solution for subatomic chaos and massive emptiness was light. Once light was introduced into the cosmos, God began to shape creation by the sound of His voice. The visible realm emerged at the speed and energy of light as a manifestation of His imagination.

You might ask, "Kris, where are you going with all this?" I am pointing out that you cannot separate real science from God, because everything created reveals the Creator. But one of the greatest challenges of the twentieth and twenty-first centuries is that science has developed an anti-God agenda. This means that scientists are studying creation with a presupposition that there is no Creator, no divine design and no purpose. These scientists must therefore devise alternative definitions, explanations, rationalizations and justifications for their exploration.

The challenge for modern scientists is much like the first-century religious leaders who spent their lives searching for God, but didn't recognize Him when He was standing right in front of them doing miracles. Science always points to the Creator, so if you ignore the reality of God, then your science becomes a religion lacking truth. It becomes a fake reality, the world absent of light, formless and void.

The good news is that God is raising up His people, infusing them with spiritual intelligence and giving them access to His mind. He is unlocking the secrets of creation held in the vaults of heaven from the eon of the ages. The knowledge of the glory of the Lord is going to cover the earth as the waters cover the sea.

11

The Law of Spiritual Physics

When a person experienced a miracle, healing or deliverance in the Gospels, the Bible called those "signs" (see John 4:49–54 for one example). The reason miracles are signs is rooted in the *way* miracles actually take place. Jesus described the dynamic with the statement that the Kingdom of heaven had come near (see Matthew 10:5–8). A superior ecosystem had superimposed itself over an inferior ecosystem, resulting in an altered physical condition. So what we call a miracle is actually a manifestation of the superior laws of third-heaven physics (called the law of the Spirit), superimposed over the inferior laws of first-heaven physics.

The apostle Paul makes this profound observation: "Therefore there is now no condemnation for those who are in Christ Jesus. For the *law of the Spirit of life* in Christ Jesus has set you free from the law of sin and of death" (Romans 8:1–2, emphasis added). The reason why we are no longer condemned, living with a death sentence under a slave master called "sin," is because of the *law of the Spirit*, with which Jesus freed us. The truth is that the spirit realm operates with laws superior to the laws of physics (for example, in this case freedom as opposed to slavery), but these laws are no less systematized, organized and structured than the laws of physics. Understanding the *law* of the Spirit is paramount to being successful in the *life* of the Spirit.

First-Heaven Physics

Let's examine the first-heaven reality of the laws of physics, for instance the law of gravity. Here is the official definition of *gravity*: "a law stating that any two masses attract each other with a force equal to a constant (constant of gravitation) multiplied by the product of the two masses and divided by the square of the distance between them."* For our illustration, we will use the simpler definition: "What goes up must come down." If I jump off a roof, there is no negotiating with the manifestation of gravity. I don't sometimes go up instead of down; it doesn't happen that 90 percent of the time I fall to the ground, but 10 percent of the time I don't. *No!* It's a law. There is no reasoning with it; it's not personal.

Now let's consider the law of lift. Here is one definition of *lift*: "Lift is a mechanical aerodynamic force produced by the motion of the airplane through the air. . . . Lift acts through the center of pressure of the object and is directed perpendicular to the flow direction."† For our purposes, let's just simplify the definition to say, "The law of lift overcomes the law of gravity and causes a plane (or many other objects) to rise instead of fall." Again, it's a law, so it's impersonal and also nonnegotiable. Can you imagine boarding a plane if lift were not a law, but rather were a relationship with the elements based on trust or some other human character quality? But it isn't. It is actually a dynamic rooted in physics that God set in motion when He created the world.

* Dictionary.com, s.v. "Law of Gravitation," Dictionary.com, LLC, 2020, https://www.dictionary.com/browse/law-of-gravitation.

† "What Is Lift?", Nancy Hall, ed., National Aeronautics and Space Administration online, May 5, 2015, https://www.grc.nasa.gov/www/k-12/airplane/lift1.html.

With this in mind, let me illustrate the *law of the Spirit* by contrasting the law of lift with the law of gravity. The law of gravity dictates that everything falls toward the earth, but the law of lift is greater than the law of gravity, in that it overcomes the law of gravity by causing objects to rise through employing a superior force.

Let's apply this to SQ. Think about a miracle, which is a sign because a superior law of the Spirit has been superimposed over an inferior law of physics, metaphorically speaking, in the same way that the law of lift overcomes the law of gravity.

"Kris, why don't we just say God did a miracle?" you ask. Because it is important to understand that a miracle is the manifestation of the third heaven's *superior* law of the Spirit. It also helps us grasp the fact that miracles are not *primarily* personal, but are much more like the law of lift, the results of which are predetermined ramifications of our actions. Yes, God set all the laws of nature in motion in every realm, so He deserves all the glory for every dimension of life, but laws are essentially nonnegotiable.

Let's examine a foundational law of the Spirit and see if my explanation begins to make sense. Jesus said, "Give, and it will be given to you. They will pour into your lap a good measure—pressed down, shaken together, and running over. For by your standard of measure it will be measured to you in return" (Luke 6:38). Two of the laws of generosity are at work in the Spirit here: (1) If you give, it will be given to you, and (2) by your measure, it will be measured to you.

God has set up a system of spiritual laws that govern generosity. If you give, God has predetermined by His Word (the same way He spoke the heavens and earth into existence) that it will return in equal measure to you, but multiplied several times over. For example, metaphorically speaking, if you give someone a teaspoon of gold nuggets in the name of Jesus, God has ordained that a teaspoon (your measure) will be used to give you a return on your investment—let's suppose ten teaspoons in return. If you give someone a gallon of gold nuggets in the name of Jesus, God has ordained that a gallon (your measure) will be the size of the vessel used to give you a return on your heavenly investment—let's say a ten-gallon return.

Let me also point out that God designed the law of prosperity in the Spirit to begin with *give*. That way, nobody is powerless or at a disadvantage, waiting to *receive* something so the process of prosperity can begin. If this law were *receive* and then *give*, we all would be powerless to activate it until we first were given something. Our entrance into the ecosystem of the Spirit would then be dependent on someone else's actions. But it isn't! We all choose when we will, by our act of generosity, engage in the law of lift (i.e., prosperity), which overcomes the law of gravity (i.e., poverty).

Why am I calling these dynamics laws? Because they are not personal; they are predicated on actions, not attitude or character. Furthermore, if you are not spiritually intelligent and you don't understand the laws of the Spirit, then you can become a victim of the invisible realm. These laws of the Spirit are so written on the hearts of our inner man that even non-Christians recognize them. For instance, some of the Eastern religions have pirated this law of prosperity and call it karma; they describe it with phrases like "whatever goes around comes around." But it is not a cult principle. It is a spiritual law taught in the Scriptures, often by Jesus Himself!

The Law of Faith

This next story personifies the law of the Spirit that we are discussing. Jesus went up the Mount of Transfiguration with His three closest disciples, namely Peter, James and John, leaving the other nine less spiritual disciples to wait at the base of the mountain. I am sure this did nothing to help put to rest the "who is the greatest?" argument among them. When the four returned from the mountaintop experience, a crowd was waiting for Jesus. A man broke through the crowd, fell on his knees and began begging Jesus to help his extremely demonized son. The man proclaimed,

"I brought him to Your disciples, and they could not cure him" (Matthew 17:16).

I can imagine that the nine left-behinds, already feeling some sense of rejection in that they were not invited to the mountain meeting, wanted to run into a cave and disappear. Remember, Jesus had asked the same nine disciples to leave the room a few days earlier, when He had raised the synagogue official's daughter from the dead (see Luke 8:49–56). Jesus' response is brutal when He hears this desperate father's request about his demonized son: "You unbelieving and perverted generation, how long shall I be with you? How long shall I put up with you?" (Matthew 17:17).

I kind of imagine the three musketeers (Peter, James and John) snickering in the background as Jesus gives the other nine a tongue-lashing. What happens next feels like one of those scenes right out of the movies, where Jesus says, "Here, Matthew, hold my glass; I'll be right back!" Jesus went on to drive out the demon and heal the kid, while the failed disciples watched in complete humiliation.

As soon as they ditched the crowd, His nine failed followers were in His face, asking, "Why could we not drive it out?" (Matthew 17:19). Jesus' response is stunning. He proclaims, "Because of the littleness of your faith; for truly I say to you, if you have faith the size of a mustard seed, you will say to this mountain, 'Move from here to there,' and it will move; and nothing will be impossible to you" (verse 20).

It almost sounds as if Jesus is saying to the nine, "It only takes a mustard seed of faith, and you nine disappointments—your faith is smaller than that!" (While He demonstrates by pretending to hold something smaller than a mustard seed between His two fingers, and then squinting His eyes to see it.) But actually, that isn't the case here. The word *littleness* in this passage is the Greek word *oligos*, meaning "brief." It does not refer to the amount of faith they had (we have); instead, it denotes how long they (we) hang on to their (our) faith in the midst of the fight. In other words, it doesn't take much faith, just a mustard seed, to move a mountain, but it does take persistent faith!

The Foundation of All SQ

Everything in the spirit realm works by the *law of faith*, whether someone is operating from the dark side (the second heaven) or from God's Spirit (the third heaven). Faith is the foundational element of everything in the spirit world.

In fact, what gravity is to the natural realm, faith is to the spirit realm. The Hebrew writer described it like this: "Now faith is the assurance of things hoped for, the conviction of things not seen" (Hebrews 11:1). He went on to say, "By faith we understand that the worlds were prepared by the word of God, so that what is seen was not made out of things which are visible" (verse 3).

This is profound. The invisible became visible by the force of faith. This means that the way we transfer things from the third heaven to the visible world is through the law of faith. This is the ultimate revelation of spiritual intelligence, the way things transfigure from ethereal, spiritual hypotheses to tangible, dynamic realities.

Furthermore, faith is the foundation of spiritual intelligence, the holy grail of the mystery of creation. We have all heard the idiom, "That guy is so heavenly minded that he's no earthly good!" Actually, the reason some spiritual people are no earthly good is that they are dreamers with no faith. It is faith that actualizes dreams, on-ramps visions and overcomes visible obstacles.

Faith Transcends the Elements

Do you remember when Jesus put His disciples in a boat and sent them to the other side of the Sea of Galilee? Later on, He came trotting out on the water in the midst of a bad storm. The guys saw Him, thought He was a ghost and freaked out. Jesus spoke to them, saying, "Take courage; it is I, do not be afraid" (Matthew 14:27). Peter suddenly had this brilliant idea and yelled, "Lord, if it is You, command me to come to You on the water" (verse 28).

You have to admit, the guy's got guts! Yet on the surface, Peter doesn't ever seem to be the sharpest knife in the drawer. I mean, if a ghost can talk to you from the water, certainly he can tell you to "come." Yet Peter possesses a special kind of spiritual intelligence that is rooted in faith and inspired by courage. The rest of the story is powerful (see more in Matthew 14:22–33). Jesus shouted, "Come!" Peter, hearing the command above the howling wind and crashing seas, got out of the boat and walked on water!

I love how Peter refuses to be satisfied with spiritual principles that have no practical application. Instead, he gets out of the dang boat while eleven theologians watch from the deck. This is it for me—the main point of this book—that someone actually steps out of the boat and attempts to walk on the sea! What good is spiritual intelligence if it has no purpose? I have observed that radical faith is so convicting to doubters, the lukewarm, the halfhearted and the religious who have re-scripted the Bible in a way that requires them to live only in the realm of reason. The truth is, you have to either be the next one out of the boat or find some spiritual excuse to relieve your cowardliness.

Peter's first water walk reminds me of the story of the Wright brothers, who were pastor's kids. On December 17, 1903, Orville Wright—after he and his brother had crashed five other planes—made the first successful plane flight in the history of the world. Only seven people were present that day to witness the historic flight, because Orville and his brother, Wilbur, had failed so many times before. The plane flew just twelve seconds at a place called Kill Devil Hills!

Like that maiden flight, Peter's water walk did not last long. Here's the rest of the story: "But seeing the wind, he became frightened, and beginning to sink, he cried out, 'Lord, save me!' Immediately Jesus stretched out His hand and took hold of him, and said to him, 'You of little faith, why did you doubt?'" (Matthew 14:30–31). If Peter had little faith, I am not sure what level of faith the eleven world changers watching from the deck had. I would also like to point out that Peter did not drown; he walked back to the boat while holding hands with Jesus.

It's important that we don't miss the main message of this story: Faith caused Peter to tap into the third-heaven, superior law of the Spirit. However brief the moment, the guy accomplished a physically impossible feat by having faith in God, which allowed him to experience the Kingdom come near him. The guy actually walked on water, demonstrating that faith is the on-ramp to experiencing a superior ecosystem manifesting over an inferior ecosystem.

We can't grow our faith on the deck of a ship. We can watch other water walkers, hear their stories and read their books, but ultimately, the only way we are going to grow our water-walking faith is to *get out of the dang boat!*

Olive

Unfortunately, Christians today often proactively cultivate a culture of unbelief in the name of wisdom. Twenty-first-century Christians are often more concerned about being sophisticated hipsters than radical Jesus followers. I have never witnessed more of a culture clash among believers than in the month of December 2019, when Olive, the two-year-old daughter of Kalley and Andrew Heiligenthal, died suddenly. Kalley, who is a worship leader in our church and part of the Bethel Music community, and Andrew, her amazing husband, immediately felt that God was going to raise Olive from the dead. They asked if the Bethel community could fast and pray for the resurrection of their daughter, worshiping and pressing in for a miracle.

The Bethel Leadership Team agreed to join these parents in faith for the resurrection of their daughter. We reasoned that it is our responsibility as believers who are earthbound to inspire the departed to return to their finite dwelling, because our Lord demonstrates it. In fact, in the Gospels we never see Jesus encountering a dead person He does not raise, nor do we see Him attending a funeral He does not ruin. Whether it was making wine from water for a wedding, or calling the deceased out of their tombs, Jesus was a walking vortex of supernatural power at every public gathering. So the war was on!

Furthermore, a couple of decades earlier we had experienced a young man named Charlie coming back to life. He had died in an accident at work and was pronounced dead on arrival at the hospital; he was showing no brain waves whatsoever. His family refused to give up and had him transported to a larger hospital, where they put him on life support. But he continued to have no brain activity at all. Yet there was another spiritual dynamic working in this case, as a few months earlier a prophet had called Charlie out of our congregation and told him he would be a great evangelist for the Lord. So Bill Johnson, our senior pastor, drove to the hospital and proclaimed that prophetic word over Charlie while he lay dead in his hospital bed. The next morning, Charlie was alive. In just a few days he was at our men's meeting, alive and completely well!

Charlie's story gave us faith that it could happen again with Olive. We sent out a call for resurrection prayer to our network of followers on our social media pages, and the number who joined us quickly reached 35 million believers from nearly every country of the world. Hundreds of thousands of Christians joined the battle remotely as they viewed some portions of the resurrection prayer and worship gatherings on social media. For five days we worshiped, prayed and proclaimed, "Olive, wake up! Come back from the dead!"

To be clear, Olive remained in the morgue, while we gathered in the sanctuary to pray. Every meeting was packed to the walls and was filled with intense prayer and worship that often lasted deep into the next morning. Kalley led worship several times during the gatherings, spontaneously taking the stage and joining the teams. Her worship was electric, exuberant and radical. She didn't just worship; instead, like a military general, she led us into battle with radical courage and divine direction, oftentimes dancing wildly as she sang.

Many leaders flew in from around the world to join us in the fray. This atmosphere created the deepest sense of camaraderie and connection both to God and to each other that I have ever experienced. Soon the secular media began to cover the story, inciting a firestorm of media requests for interviews. Within days, more than 35 news agencies, including Fox News, *USA Today* and CNN, were covering our quest for Olive to rise from the dead. I'm sure you can imagine some of the responses as unbelievers tried to wrap their finite minds around our infinite request from heaven. We were contending for a miracle, something that defies the laws of nature. We knew it was irrational in this realm, but we understood that "nothing is impossible with God."

There was another deeply troubling camp that emerged in the fray as we contended for Olive's resurrection—unbelieving Christians. Hundreds of them began to rise up against us with biblical arguments about why we should stop the resurrection prayer gatherings. It might be important to understand that Bethel Church has been around for 63 years and we have never had a dead-raising prayer service for anyone in our history, but we have had hundreds of funerals. So resurrection services are not our norm. Furthermore, it was not Bethel leadership's idea to initiate these miracle services. It was Kalley and Andrew's idea, who had requested that we join them in faith. All of this to say that I totally understand that believing for God to raise the dead is rare, radical and even intellectually irrational. But it is also biblically sound!

My concern is that unbelief has become the prominent culture among Christians. Not only do we not get out of the boat ourselves; we also create elaborate theologies against water walking, and we persecute the Peters of the faith. We deafen ourselves to the voice of the Lord, who says "Come!" to each of us. Yet Kalley and Andrew are right; the Scriptures are on their side. Here is one of the biblical accounts:

These twelve Jesus sent out after instructing them: "Do not go in the way of the Gentiles, and do not enter any city of the Samaritans; but rather go to the lost sheep of the house of Israel. And as you go, preach, saying, 'The kingdom of heaven is at hand.' Heal the sick, raise the dead, cleanse the lepers, cast out demons. Freely you received, freely give."

Matthew 10:5–8

Some Christians are so obstinate. "Well," they conclude, "Jesus told His twelve disciples to raise the dead, but He didn't tell us to."

Seriously? First, no one told Peter to walk on water. There was no command to do it, no Scripture that said he should, and Jesus did not even instruct him to do so. But Peter saw Jesus walking on water and figured He was demonstrating what was possible for everyone, so he asked to join Him. Furthermore, Jesus' words in all four gospels were spoken to other people, but we still apply them to ourselves. Jesus said "love your neighbor as yourself" to a crowd of first-century people, not to us. Does anyone ever make the argument, "That was for *those* folks, not for us"? And finally, there were more than ten raisings of the dead in the Bible, three of them in the Old Testament, before Jesus rose from the dead and gave us power from on high (see Acts 1:8). But the greatest evidence that we should be raising the dead is that Jesus Himself did it, and then He said this:

Truly, truly, I say to you, he who believes in Me, the works that I do, he will do also; and greater works than these he will do; because I go to the Father. Whatever you ask in My name, that will I do, so that the Father may be glorified in the Son. If you ask Me anything in My name, I will do it.

John 14:12–14

"Extraordinary!" you say. Yes, but this is the call of true spiritual intelligence. It is not just that believers have access to information that no one else has; it is that we also have power that the world has yet to experience.

Hope Deferred

Then there are those who presented a compassionate argument for not believing for a miracle. Their comment was, "We don't want to create false hope in these people by having them believe that their child will come to life!"

On the surface this sounds logical and caring, but it is completely absent of faith. What if Olive did rise? Or what if her parents had done nothing and she didn't rise, but after they buried her, they kept feeling she would have risen if they had believed? Have you ever felt a conviction you didn't act on, and then regretted it later? Acting on your convictions is the life of faith! Peter got out of the boat. He did it! He tried, but ultimately failed—or did he?

The other thing that makes me crazy is that we rarely apply this "false hope" test to the medical community. When someone has a terminal disease, sometimes the doctor says, "There's a new treatment that might work; it has worked on a few people." I have never heard anyone say in response, "That doctor is creating false hope in his patient." How many times have we heard of a cancer patient traveling to Mexico, Spain or Germany for treatments that aren't legal in America? These international treatments may not cure a lot of people, but they give desperate people hope.

Maybe the most important point about hope is that it is the seed-bed of faith—meaning you cannot have faith without hope. Remember the verse we looked at earlier: "Now faith is the assurance of things hoped for, the conviction of things not seen" (Hebrews 11:1). Hope feels, faith sees and love never fails!

The gravity of all the laws of the Spirit rests on faith, yet you cannot have faith without first experiencing hope. Hope feels; it doesn't see. It is the earnest expectation that something good is about to happen. Hope does not know what's going to happen; it just knows something will.

Once hope creates expectation, faith begins to "look" for the thing hope is feeling. Hope is like the great smell coming from the kitchen; faith is seeing the steak. Hope is hearing the car coming up the driveway; faith is getting up to see your daughter whom you haven't heard from in two years coming up your driveway.

"Don't get your hopes up" is the motto of unbelievers (and unbelieving Christians). The believers' creed is, "Get your hopes up; something good is about to *happen*!" The writer of the book of Hebrews exhorted us with these words: "Without faith, it is impossible to please Him, for he who comes to God must believe that He is and that He is a rewarder of those who seek Him" (Hebrews 11:6).

The Fight for Hope

About two weeks after Olive died, we put her little body to rest in a grave in our community. It was a heart-wrenching punch to the gut for everyone who had prayed and really believed. Together, we had stepped out of the boat, but just a little way from the vessel we sank, all of us in it together. We didn't blame God, nor did we question our faith or our process. Instead, together we embraced the mystery of God's goodness.

At the funeral we sang songs about the goodness of God, while Kalley and Andrew led us with reckless abandon. Solomon wrote, "Hope deferred makes the heart sick, but desire fulfilled is a tree of life" (Proverbs 13:12). It is not deferring what we hoped for that makes our hearts sick; it is deferring our *hope* that makes us sick. When we stop hoping, we get sick.

The road ahead will be painful for Kalley, Andrew and our team. But we live to try again. Together, we will come into the next battle with even more fervency. We are believers, and we all understood the risks we were taking when we stepped out of the boat and attempted to walk on water. We knew we would be criticized for believing the impossible in the midst of what seemed inevitable, but that is what we forerunners do.

I love what Theodore Roosevelt said:

It is not the critic who counts; not the man who points out how the strong man stumbles, or where the doer of deeds could have done them better. The credit belongs to the man who is actually in the arena, whose face is marred by dust and sweat and blood; who strives valiantly; who errs, who comes short again and again . . . who knows great enthusiasms, the great devotions; who spends himself in a worthy cause; who at the best knows in the end the triumph of high achievement, and who, at the worst, if he fails, at least fails while daring greatly, so that his place shall never be with those timid souls who neither know victory nor defeat.*

Personally, I would rather die in faith than live in doubt! I want to invite you to step out of the boat, and together we will meet on the water.

More to Learn

There is so much to learn about the laws of the Spirit that literally fill the Bible—statements like humble yourself and you will be exalted at the proper time (see 1 Peter 5:16). Or like ask and it will be given to you; seek and you will find; knock and the door will be opened to you (see Matthew 7:7). Yet all these impersonal spiritual laws fly on the wings of faith. In fact, everything in the spirit world rides on faith.

Why didn't Olive rise from the dead? I honestly have no idea, but chances are that if Jesus had shown up in the flesh, we would not have had a funeral. Is faith the only factor in raising the dead, or in any miracle, for that matter? I'm not sure, but it's obviously the primary factor for miracles, since nearly every time the disciples failed at their assignment, Jesus would ask them questions like "Where is your faith?" or "Do you still not believe?"

---

* This special excerpt called "The Man in the Arena" passage is from Theodore Roosevelt's speech "Citizenship in a Republic," which he delivered at the Sorbonne in Paris, France, on April 23, 1910.

Part of the challenge is that you *always believe*. If you *don't believe* that the person you are praying for is going to get healed, for example, then you actually have *faith* that the person *will not* get healed. In other words, your unbelief is actually a faith force, in that you believed nothing would happen, and therefore it turned out according to your faith.

Job put it like this: "For what I fear comes upon me, and what I dread befalls me" (Job 3:25). Job's statement shows us that fear is an act of faith—faith in the wrong kingdom! Think about it: You can't have fear without faith. For example, if a little boy tells you he is going to beat you up, his words create no anxiety in you because you don't believe him. But if some Mafia gangster uses those same words, you're probably going to experience some fear because you believe he can hurt you. The real challenge is that failure can become a culture.

Proactive Faith

Let me share a story that will clarify what I am saying. Years ago, I had a friend I'll call Dan who was sitting at a stoplight when a guy plowed into the back of his car. The accident destroyed his vehicle and really messed up his neck. Dan was off work for weeks, dealing with the pain. Just as he was getting well, he got hit again at another stoplight, with a similar outcome. Afterward he said, "I was afraid this would happen to me again."

The crazy thing was, Dan was in his forties and had never been in an auto accident in his entire life. But the story gets worse. Within the next couple of years he was in nearly half a dozen more accidents, and none of them happened while his car was moving.

It's probably obvious, but the worst thing about Dan's first car accident is that it attracted a foreboding spirit (the word *foreboding* means a sense of impending doom). He began to fear an accident would happen again. And because fear is actually a manifestation of faith, every time an accident happened, his faith grew for it to happen again!

One of the things I have learned about spiritual intelligence over the years is that it matters how I deal with defeat, because defeats can give me faith for a life of failure. But I can also choose to live with a proactive faith. When I look at an experience like Olive's in the same way that the Wright brothers viewed their five previous airplane crashes—each attempt making them more determined to learn and try again, until they actually flew—I begin to see faith as more of a journey than a destination. Spiritual intelligence is a lifelong process that daily brings me closer to God. I want to encourage you to find closure for your defeats so that you find victory in your daily life.

12

Creativity, Invention and Innovation

There are so many dimensions to SQ, which means there are so many boats we need to exit, so much water just waiting to be walked on and so much of nature longing for a transcended experience with God. Literally, the natural world is coaxing us out of the boat of boring living and imploring us to discover the secrets of the universe.

This was really driven home in my heart one winter a few years back. A young kid came up to where I was sitting in the front of the church and handed me a gift-wrapped present. He stood there eagerly, waiting impatiently as I unwrapped the gift. When I finally managed to get it open (it was wrapped as if it were a national treasure), I realized it contained six blister-packed magnets shaped like two-inch donuts. This kid opened the see-through package for me and demonstrated how fun it was to play with the magnets. We both laughed as we embraced. Evidently, he had heard a message in which I talked about my inability to be present with people unless I do something trivial with my hands, so he thought the magnets would do the trick for me. I thanked him and put them in my pants pocket.

I carried those magnets around for so long that only two of them survived the brutal beating of the washing machine. The ones that endured were so badly chipped that I finally threw them away one day. But as I left work, I felt convicted about the magnets, so I rescued the silly things from the garbage can. That night, I had a dream about the secret of magnetism being revealed to the world, so I continued to carry those magnets with me for several more months while I tried to figure out what to do with them.

Finally, a friend of mine introduced me through email to a wealthy businessman, who asked if I would have dinner with him when I was in Los Angeles for a conference. I agreed, and the next month a limo picked me up at my LA hotel and took me to Mastro's Steakhouse in Beverly Hills. When I arrived, the businessman and one of his associates were waiting for me outside. We greeted each other and took a seat at a beautiful round table. I spent the first hour trying to discern what I was doing there, as the goal of the meeting was a little unclear to me. The gentleman inquired a lot about my experience with the prophetic ministry and how he might grow his own gift.

About an hour passed, and still knowing very little about his business ventures or his life, I precipitously felt as if I was supposed to take the magnets out of my pocket and play with them on the table. I have to admit, I felt a little stupid playing with magnets on the table of an exclusive restaurant while a wealthy businessman I hardly knew watched.

I said, "John [not his real name], check this out." I took the magnets and showed him. "Do you see that?" I asked.

He nodded yes.

"That's magnetic power, and it's going to transform the world! But here is the best news, John. God is going to give *you* the secret of magnetic power, and you're going to become the richest man in the world!" I prophesied.

"Do you know anything about me?" he inquired.

"I know you're a wealthy businessman, but I don't know anything else, not even what kind of businesses you have," I answered.

"That's interesting. I own several companies, and one of them is a magnetic invention and innovation company that hasn't ever been profitable. I had decided to close it down, but before doing so, I thought I should ask God if He had a view. I have been praying about it for the past several months. I was just in the process of selling it off this month. I guess I'll have to keep it now," he said, chuckling.

I gave him the magnets as a prophetic sign, kind of like Joshua stacking up rocks in the river Jordan.

Fast-forward three years, to not long ago. John again had a limo pick me up from my LA hotel and this time take me to the Spago restaurant for another meeting. By now, I had come to know John and his associates a little more, as we had met casually a few times at different events. I have to admit, I was a little anxious about the meeting, having given John such a significant word about God revealing to him the secret of magnetism. Soon I was seated at a table with John, his associates and their spouses. Moments passed, and my fear was dispatched by the faith I could feel tangibly emanating from John and his team. John began to recount to me how his company had invented a magnetic motor that was the most energy efficient motor in the history of the world! He went on to explain that the field of aviation would see the first application of the motor, as they soon would begin installing them into planes. Just recently, John sent me a note that read, "Hi, Kris—*You are the father of a new era of transportation!*"

The Father of Invention

John and his team are prototypes of individuals who are forging ahead in spiritual intelligence, tapping into creativity, invention and innovation. This should not surprise us. Many of the greatest inventors of the past centuries were believers inspired by the Holy Spirit to discover and create.

As we talked about earlier, it was on December 17, 1903, that Orville and Wilbur Wright, after crashing five other planes, made the first successful plane flight in the history of the world. Yet an often overlooked fact is that the Wright brothers were pastor's kids. Their father, Bishop Milton Wright, and his wife, Susan, raised their boys to be dreamers! The Wright brothers credited their inspiration for flight to a toy helicopter that their father bought them on one of his road trips.

Unfortunately, unlike Orville, Wilbur or my friend John, many Christians live with limited, powerless, finite thinking. How is this even possible? How do people who claim to have the Creator of the universe living inside them, the mind of Christ thinking through them, and the Spirit of God influencing the world around them even have the nerve to think small?

I would propose that we believers don't have permission to live with limited mindsets, because God is the Father of invention!

Unbelieving Believers

I love Elon Musk. Although Musk doesn't profess to believe in God, he thinks like Him! How is this even possible? Musk sat on the LA freeway in bumper-to-bumper traffic, frustrated by "this enormous waste of time." As he pondered his situation, he began to dream of ways to solve the transportation dilemma that has plagued Southern Californians forever. He envisioned a maze of hyperloop tunnels bored at various levels underneath the city of Los Angeles to connect people to their ultimate destination.

I mean, when I sit in traffic, I wonder, *What's on the radio?* I have never thought about solving the LA traffic problem with a space-age hyperloop system. And that's the problem!

Furthermore, Musk didn't just dream about a hyperloop system; he is constructing it. That's right—a few years later, through much red tape, near-miraculous inventions, and at the estimated cost of billions of dollars, Musk is now boring his first tunnels under his SpaceX parking lot. If successful, the tunnel system will become a true superhighway that will literally put our cars on a roller skate and thrust us through the earth's crust at 120 miles per hour!

"Crazy!" you say? This is just one of Musk's most insignificant endeavors. This guy wants to colonize Mars (yes, the planet), "making humanity a multiplanetary species," by the year 2040.

"Daydreamer!" you say? Maybe so, but he has already invented and built the most powerful rocket ever created in the history of the world. And, oh, by the way, the rocket is reusable. Musk doesn't believe in God, but he does believe in doing the impossible. He is what I call an unbelieving believer!

Cultures That Cultivate Clones

One of the reasons why Elon Musk thinks like a believer, and why many Christians think like unbelievers, is that we Christians can have a terrible fear of thinking. In contrast, he has developed a culture of creativity in and around him. Cultures matter. Great cultures are the divine x factor, the difference maker, the tangible yet sometimes unexplainable "sense" of empowerment and inspiration. In my mind, our problem is twofold—rooted in the way we view the Bible and in our deep-seated fear of deception. Let's look at each of these challenges a little more closely.

Our first challenge begins with the way we view the Bible. For many Christians, the Scriptures are a box, a limitation and a strong boundary embodying *all truth*. Their basic Christian belief is that if it's not in the Bible, it's (for the most part) not true.

In fairness, however, nearly all Christians believe in things like air conditioning, modern transportation, electronic devices—tangible things that seem amoral (without moral value). Christians rarely let their purchases be affected by who invented, manufactured or distributed any product. Most believers are fine with enjoying inventions

147

and/or innovations created by cultists, atheists or immoral activists, as long as you don't quote those people. Quoting them on social media creates a firestorm of pushback as Christians vilify anyone embracing any of these inventors' ideas. Embracing their innovative ideas can get you labeled as deceived since the common culture of Christianity is guilt by association. This mindset creates a ton of anxiety, which ultimately robs people of creativity and derails invention and innovation.

But what if we viewed the Bible as an empowering platform instead of a limiting container? What if we viewed God as bigger than His book? Before I make you crazy, I certainly am not talking about preaching a different gospel, or that there are many ways to God, or that there is no hell, or anything remotely similar to that. Nor am I suggesting that there are other Scriptures outside the 66 books of the Bible. Furthermore, I agree that we should never embrace any idea that is anti-biblical or anti-God. I am simply pointing out that the goal of the Bible is for us to get to know God. Furthermore, the entire Bible is true, but not everything that is true is in the Bible.

For example, the laws of electricity are true. There is the equation $E = I \times R$, also known as Ohm's law, which is used to discover voltage in relation to electrical current and resistance. Or there is the equation $W = A \times V$, which is used to convert electrical current in amps to electrical current in watts. But true although they are, you will not find these in the pages of the Bible. The laws of physics are true as well, but they are not in the Bible either. I would like to propose that God created the principles of electricity and the laws of physics, but He did not explain them in the Scriptures. Yet understanding these laws and principles is the foundation for all modern invention and innovation.

The second challenge many Christians face that destroys high levels of thinking is their deep-seated fear of being deceived. Christians often have more faith in the devil's ability to deceive them than they have faith in the Holy Spirit's ability to lead them.

Of course, these fears are not completely irrational or unfounded. There are some very good reasons to be concerned about deception. I understand that Christian history is riddled with the dead spiritual bones of radical believers who went off to universities, Hollywood or some other place of "higher learning," only to return as liberal critics of the Kingdom. But we must realize that creative thinking is in our DNA, and it is therefore part of God's nature in every believer.

R&D Cultures

What's the answer? Let me respond by contrasting two cultures and explaining how these must be held in proper tension to create a healthy culture of character that inspires spiritual intelligence. I call this contrast the *production* versus the *R&D* (research and development) tension. I liken the idea of *production* to our character, sound doctrine and relationship with God and people. I equate *R&D* to revelation, invention, innovation and creativity.

Let me explain this with a short business analysis. When Apple Corporation went to market with its new iPhone, the goal of the manufacturing (production) department was to have no defects whatsoever show up in the phones they were selling. But the research and development department, which invented the iPhone, made hundreds of mistakes in the process of developing the product. If Apple had tried to apply the same core values to the R&D department as it did to the manufacturing division, the R&D teams never would have invented any products.

In other words, even though both these divisions are part of the same great company, success in the two departments is measured much differently. Mistakes are the inevitable process of invention, but they are the demise of production. The same is true of the business of our inner man. Lying, cheating, rage and immorality are just a few examples of "production" core values that we cannot and should not tolerate. On the other hand, learning to hear the voice of God, moving in miracles, interpreting dreams and visions, and healing the sick are all examples of "R&D" activities that deserve gracious core values allowing us to step out in faith, without fear of punishment or reprisal.

For instance, if we view a person who gets a word of knowledge wrong as a "false prophet" or someone having a "false prophecy," we certainly won't create a very empowering culture. On the other hand, if we teach people how to grow in spiritual intelligence, and if we handle wrong prophetic words as mistakes made by individuals who are learning and developing their gifts, then we will have a great R&D culture that inspires participation.

What's Spiritual?

Sometimes when we think of spirituality, we envision some dude sitting on the floor with his legs crossed, rocking back and forth, humming to himself. But nothing could be further from the truth. As a matter of fact, the very first person in the entire Bible ever to be filled with the Spirit was a craftsman named Bezalel. The Spirit literally gave him the supernatural ability for creativity. Check out the conversation between God and Moses as He explains the situation to his servant:

> Now the LORD spoke to Moses, saying, "See, I have called by name Bezalel, the son of Uri, the son of Hur, of the tribe of Judah. I have filled him with the Spirit of God in wisdom, in understanding, in knowledge, and in all kinds of craftsmanship, to make artistic designs for work in gold, in silver, and in bronze, and in the cutting of stones for settings, and in the carving of wood, that he may work in all kinds of craftsmanship."
>
> Exodus 31:1–5

God gave Moses comprehensive instructions for a cool building called the Tabernacle of Moses, right down to the smallest detail.

It was to be incredibly beautiful, with hand-carved statues and pillars, lots of brightly colored materials, and loads of gold, silver and bronze. But the building was so complex and ornate that Moses' greatest challenge was finding skilled people who could actually build the thing.

Did I mention that Moses' entire workforce was made up of former slaves who knew nothing about creativity? How would God solve this seemingly impossible situation? He simply filled a guy with His Spirit, giving him the ability to do natural things in a supernatural way.

Work Is Spiritual

God is redefining spirituality. Years ago, I realized that when I received Jesus, I became part of a "royal priesthood" (1 Peter 2:9), and from that day forward, I was no longer working a secular job. I suddenly recognized that the King lives in me; therefore, everything I do is for the King's domain (the Kingdom) and is subsequently sacred. When I "offered my body to God as a living sacrifice, which is my spiritual service of worship" (see Romans 12:1), the outcome of my radical sacrifice was that it caused my body to become an instrument of worship.

I was an automotive technician when I received this revelation. One day I realized that what the guitar was to the worship leader on Sunday mornings, my wrenches and screwdrivers were to me throughout the week, because I was anointed by the Spirit to repair cars for the glory of God. I was in the ministry for years and never knew it.

There is no such thing as laymen in the Kingdom; there is only a royal priesthood. All believers are therefore priests. Repairing cars became spiritual warfare because I was fulfilling the call of God on my life.

There is a great story in the Bible about the servants of the devil (represented as horns) warring against God's people. And whom does God send to thwart the attack and destroy the works of the devil? Four craftsmen!

> Then I lifted up my eyes and looked, and behold, there were four horns. So I said to the angel who was speaking with me, "What are these?" And he answered me, "These are the horns which have scattered Judah, Israel and Jerusalem." Then the LORD showed me four craftsmen. I said, "What are these coming to do?" And he said, "These are the horns which have scattered Judah so that no man lifts up his head; but these craftsmen have come to terrify them, to throw down the horns of the nations who have lifted up their horns against the land of Judah in order to scatter it."
>
> Zechariah 1:18–21

When we do what the Spirit has anointed us to do, we are not just helping people; we are also terrorizing the enemy. It is so important that we find our place of calling in life, and that we understand that each of us is born to be an instrument of God, filled with the Spirit of God, to do the works of God.

13

Doing Business with God

In 1978, we moved from the Bay Area to a town of about nine hundred people called Lewiston, nestled in the Trinity Alps of Northern California. Times were tough, as I was in the middle of a nervous breakdown that ultimately lasted three years. To make matters worse, we had spent all our money buying and fixing up an old mountain cabin, so we were pretty broke. This inspired us to get up early in the morning and make our way down to the river near our house, with our baby and two dogs in tow, to fish for food. I was working as a shop manager at Trinity Tire, a tire store in Weaverville, a town about fifteen miles from our house. My goal was to be the pastor of a church someday.

In late 1979, a prophet named Dick Mills came to our little Assembly of God church to minister on a Sunday morning. After the service, several of us took him out to lunch. During the meal, Dick gave all of us prophetic words. He turned to me and said, "God is going to give you double wisdom for business; the wisdom of man and the wisdom of God."

I left the restaurant distraught. "I want to be in the ministry!" I protested to Kathy. She reassured me that God knew what He was doing.

The next night, we had a friend of ours named Patrick over for dinner. The mood was light as we ate, told jokes and laughed together. Suddenly, Patrick's countenance shifted, as if he were taken over by the Holy Spirit. He looked at me and proclaimed in a loud voice, "God says if you will open a business, He will bless you!"

Without hesitation I protested, "I don't want to go into business. I want to be a pastor!"

"Bro, I'm just telling you what He said to me," he responded with a stupid smile.

"Well, you tell Him what I said!" I snapped back.

That week I had our car all torn apart in the shop, so my close friend Charlie Harper picked me up for work the next morning. We made small talk on the way to work, but as we passed the Union 76 station, Charlie said, "I had a dream last night that you owned that station."

"Well, I don't want to be in business. I want to be a pastor," I explained.

Charlie (always the gracious one) agreed with my desire and reassured me of my pastoral call.

Friday of that same week rolled around, and I was up to my elbows in broken cars. The shop phone rang. With my hands covered in grease, I answered the phone in frustration, trying to make it clear to the caller that I was in a hurry.

The person on the other end of the line stopped me in my tracks by asking if I was interested in buying the Union 76 station in town. I was floored! Everything in me wanted to say, "I want to be a pastor, *not a businessman!*" But I feared in my own self-will that I could actually be fighting God, so I agreed to meet the next week to find out more about the deal.

I got home that evening and explained the situation to Kathy. She was in a totally different place than I was. She was excited about the "opportunity" and was looking forward to hearing the terms. I reassured myself that we didn't have any money (in fact, our house payment was already late), so I knew that the owner would walk away from the deal.

When we met to discuss the conditions of the sale, I found out that the owner graciously was willing to finance the purchase himself. My "I got no money" speech had only fueled his creative juices. All I had to do was put down $9,000 and make monthly payments on the rest of the loan.

When I arrived home, Kathy met me at the car, excited to hear all the details. (I never seem to ask enough questions to satisfy that girl's need-to-know brain.) When I explained that the deal required a $9,000 down payment, she immediately responded, "Ask your grandmother to lend you the money. I feel as if she's going to help us!"

I very reluctantly called my grandmother, who was not famous for her generosity. "Grandma, I want to ask you to lend me $9,000 so I can buy a service station," I eked out on the phone.

"Okay," she said in a monotone voice. "I won't lend it to you," she went on, matter-of-fact. "But I will give it to you!"

I was floored. I could hardly believe my ears. *I just got shanghaied into business by God*, I thought. *This is insane!*

I gave my notice at the tire shop the next day and my boss fired me on the spot, realizing I was about to become his competitor. I was livid! But later that day, I was able to work out a deal with the Union 76 owner to manage his station for a month until the thirty-day escrow closed and I could buy it.

All too soon, the 29th day rolled around and we were supposed to put our $9,000 in escrow. Unfortunately, we had spent $1,400 of it just running the business. Since the owner had been so good to us, we didn't want to tell him we were short. We prayed our guts out! I was angry. I told God, *This was Your idea! I wanted to be a pastor! Now we're in trouble, and I'm scared!*

The escrow company called on day thirty to remind me that we needed to have the $9,000 there by noon if we wanted the deal to happen.

"Okay, I got it handled," I responded confidently, having no idea how I was going to produce the $1,400 that we were short. A couple of hours later I was lying on a creeper, working under a truck, when a good friend of mine handed me some money. I figured he was paying for filling up with gas, so I thanked him and put it in my shirt pocket.

"Dude, you might want to take a look at that money I just gave you," he taunted.

I rolled out from under the truck and pulled the cash out of my pocket. It was fourteen brand-new $100 bills. I almost wet my pants!

"Where did you get all that money?" I pressed.

"A guy asked me to give it to you," he explained.

I was dumbfounded. How could anyone know that I needed $1,400? We had told no one.

"What the heck is happening here? I mean, I don't get it!"

Kathy and I went right down to the title company and plopped our $9,000 down on the counter, just like people who knew what they were doing. Little did we know that this would be the first month's miracle in a series of many ongoing miracles that tended to hover over our business in those years.

At a Crossroad

We grew so fast that by 1985 we had added a fleet repair shop and a foreign car shop, all in a little town of three thousand people in a county of ten thousand. One day while I was meditating and praying, I felt the Lord tell me to open an auto parts store. There were already three of them in Weaverville, but they were so poorly run that they drove all the repair shops crazy. The problem was, I had no money. We were growing so rapidly that it was taking all our cash.

Then one day, I had an encounter with the Lord. He asked me, *Do you trust Me?*

These kinds of questions always make me nervous because I know so many wild Bible stories in which people were required to do crazy things by faith. Things like prophesying to dead bones, walking on water, defeating huge armies with only three hundred men, killing a giant with a rock—the stories go on and on.

Do I trust You? Well, I think I do, was my honest response.

Then I heard the Lord tell me, *Okay, Kris, I want you to hire two countermen and put them in parts store uniforms.*

I wanted to remind the Lord that I had no parts, but I figured He knew it already. A few days later He told me, *Rent a building for the parts store.*

I honestly wasn't sure how I was going to do that, as we had *no cash*. But hey, at least God hadn't asked me to sacrifice my firstborn or something. So I looked for a small, cheap building I could fix up into a storefront, and I finally found one. The place was pretty decrepit, but it was a start. When I went to sign the lease, I heard the Lord tell me that the place was *inadequate*. I didn't sign.

A few days later, I found a great building and sat down with the landlord to tell him my situation. "I need a year of free rent so I can get my auto parts business off the ground," I said.

He looked at me sort of funny, and then said, "Okay, I'll do it!"

The only major thing I was missing was—you guessed it—auto parts. I did some research and figured out the best auto parts warehouse to buy from. I made an appointment with Dave, the warehouse's owner. I told him I needed about $100,000 worth of parts, and I shared my vision with him. He was all-in, until I told him I had no money. He got really angry, feeling I was wasting his time.

"I do have a plan," I divulged. "I have my father-in-law's solid gold watch that's a family heirloom. I'll give it to you for collateral until I pay off my auto parts bill."

"How much is that #*&@! thing worth?" he inquired.

"About $10,000," I said, trying to ignore the obvious disparity.

That sent him on a rant using several Egyptian words I can't print here. He finally said, "You're crazy! Completely nuts!"

"No, think about it. If I don't pay you, I'll have lost my family's most prized possession. How will I ever look them in the eye after such a tragedy?" I countered. The Lord had given me the idea, so I had actually brought the watch with me. I pulled the one-hundred-year-old pocket watch out of its velvet case and showed it to Dave. He was unimpressed.

"What am I going to do with that $%!&# thing?" he protested. He walked away, yelling, "I'll think about it."

I drove home discouraged. I felt embarrassed by my ridiculous plan—a $10,000 watch for $100,000 worth of inventory. *How insulting*, I mused. But the hardest part was admitting that I had misunderstood the Lord.

The days passed so slowly as I waited for Dave's response. Every day, I felt more ashamed by my dumb plan. I played the scene over and over in my mind, like a bad song you can't get out of your head.

A week passed, and finally Dave called. "I want to come up to Weaverville and see what you're $%#@& doing up there. Is later today all right with you?"

"Yep, that's great," I said (trying not to yell *hallelujah* over the phone while dancing the chicken walk).

Two hours later, Dave arrived with a couple of his managers. I watched them from my office window as they made their way across our parking lot packed with cars. The shops were all slammed as usual, and I could tell by our visitors' countenances that they were impressed. But as Dave entered the office, he put on his game face and was trying noticeably to act unimpressed. I quickly discerned that this is the way he negotiated: *Act uninterested. . . . You have nothing I want. . . . I'm the big dog; you're the little dog.* But his two managers blew his cover because they kept *ooh*ing and *aah*ing during the entire tour.

When we got to the beautiful parts store building, which we had just finished remodeling, Dave couldn't contain himself. "This is

$%*#@ nice!" he said. "What're you going to do for shelving and counters?" he inquired in a more respectful tone.

"I haven't quite figured that out yet," I humbly admitted.

"I'll give you all that stuff, and some day you can pay me something for it," he announced. "Let's get this %*$#! deal done," he continued. "I'll send a team up to set up the shelves, and we can figure out what you need for parts."

I was trying hard not to do the chicken dance right there in the building. A month later, we were in business. We called it *Crossroad Auto Parts*, and our motto was *Excellent Service, the Crossroad Difference.*

The Computer That Couldn't

The day we opened, the store was packed. We grew much faster than our financial projections had predicted, but cash was still really tight all the time. We purchased a computer system with a generic POS (point of sale) program for about $3,000. Real auto parts software started at $30,000, so it was out of the question. Selling auto parts is a unique business all its own. Besides the challenge of having millions of part numbers that we had to upload manually into our generic software system, auto parts have five price levels. Our POS system was limited to three price levels, which was not a problem until we began to win larger accounts that required deeper discounts than our funky software could calculate. The only way we could give a client a better discount was to manually override each individual part during the sale. The process was tedious, and my team would often get busy and forget the discount.

As we got busier, this problem grew worse every day. We tried everything, even having Kathy go back after closing and correct every invoice. This took her hours every night, and she would still miss some part numbers. Finally, we called the software company and explained our dilemma to the developers. They worked on the problem for more than a week and ultimately gave up. "Kris," they explained, "the software platform was only designed for three price levels. It simply can't accommodate any more levels."

I was distraught. A friend of mine knew a "top-notch software genius" who he was sure could fix it. This genius came to our parts store after hours for a week, but even he had no luck. He finally gave up, agreeing with the software designer that the machine was limited to three price levels.

Coincidentally, the next week was a disaster! Looking haggard, one of our largest shop customers came in early one morning and demanded to talk to me. My men scrambled to my office like rats in a lightning storm.

Throwing down a stack of receipts six inches high on the counter, this customer shouted, "I stayed up half the night going through every single part I purchased from you. You guys are a bunch of crooks! Every time I turn my back, you cheat me! I'm done doing business with your establishment, and I'm going to tell everyone you're a shyster."

I tried to explain the situation and of course offered to give him his discounts, but he was livid. He stomped out of the parts house, mumbling curses as he parted.

I didn't sleep much that night. I mostly prayed and meditated on all the miracles it had taken to get this far. I certainly didn't blame the customers for being angry. It looked really bad, as if our motives were evil. I finally prayed for God to give us an answer and fell asleep.

At about 3:00 a.m. I woke up with a vivid dream etched into my mind, almost like an open vision. I saw four lines of code written clearly on a piece of paper. Let me be clear that I knew nothing about our computer. Depending on your age, you may remember the old DOS system that required you to boot it up every morning. I had to wait for my manager to come in each day to turn on the system. But I hurried up and wrote the dream's code down in the journal I kept by the bed. I leaned over and woke Kathy up because she knew how to turn the computer on and she could type.

Let's just say my wife was not a happy camper. It was 4:00 a.m. by then and there was three feet of snow on the ground. But the real dilemma was trying to convince her that God had given me the answer to our POS software issue. She just was not a believer. (She believed in Jesus; it was me she was struggling with!)

I hounded Kathy until she got up, threw on her clothes and agreed to go to the parts store. It was a quiet ride. She got the computer up and sarcastically asked me to read the first line of code. I didn't know how to describe some of the characters, so she took my journal and read it herself.

Suddenly, she looked up and said, "I think we're in the back of the program! Let me put in the other three lines of code. . . ." Then she went on, "I think something happened! Let's create a dummy customer and see how many price levels are available."

Bam! Five price levels emerged! Our problem was solved. We both looked at each other in utter shock. What the software developer could not do, and what the genius could not fix, God had fixed—in a dream, no less! Kathy and I were both doing the chicken dance at 5:00 a.m. in a freezing parts store. We used that software for several more years, until we could afford an automotive parts system.

The Goal of Spiritual Intelligence

People who have little or no experience with SQ often pen so much of what is written about life in the Spirit. Many ministers travel the world and speak about ethereal philosophies that frankly they have never walked out in their own lives. Nowhere is this manifested more vigorously than on social media, where Christians are often the most vicious people on any page. Many of them incite a holy war against anyone they disagree with, and they spend hours arguing over theological ideas and wrangling over Bible verses that they dismember like a biologist dissecting a frog.

Personally, I love dialoging and even debating ideas, theorizing about Scriptures and speculating about God's divine theology. I appreciate apologists who can defend the Gospel with powerful, scriptural discourse and intelligent, logical evidence. But at the end of the day, our faith must actually *work*.

The apostle John wrote, "The Word became flesh, and dwelt among us" (John 1:14). In my mind, the ultimate test of truth is, Can you dress it up in flesh? Does it equal an experience, or is it just words, intellectual ideas or vain philosophies?

Paul was dealing with this very issue in the first-century Church in the Greek city of Corinth. The Greeks were famous for their philosophers, and the people spent a lot of time gathering in the marketplace to debate ideas. This was the television, news and social media of their day. But much like the religion of today, their conversations were rooted in theories, lofty ideas and ethereal speculations.

This culture seeped into the Church in that region, and the apostle Paul became sick of it and finally wrote the following warning: "I will come to you soon, if the Lord wills, and I shall find out, not the words of those who are arrogant but their power. For the kingdom of God does not consist in words but in power" (1 Corinthians 4:19–20).

Paul had a similar issue in the Greek city of Ephesus, where Timothy was shepherding the local Church community. Paul wrote to him,

> Solemnly charge them in the presence of God not to wrangle about words, which is useless and leads to the ruin of the hearers. Be diligent to present yourself approved to God as a workman who does not need to be ashamed, accurately handling the word of truth. But avoid worldly and empty chatter, for it will lead to further ungodliness, and their talk will spread like gangrene.
>
> 2 Timothy 2:14–17

The reason I have filled this book with "practical" stories is because it is hard to become what you have not seen or heard. It is my desire to teach people how to tap into spiritual intelligence that actually has practical applications for everyday life. It is true that a person with an argument has no power over a person with an experience!

14

What Time Is It?

My experience in business opened my eyes to understand that there are specific seasons in life for everything God has called us to. Discerning these divine epoch times in our spiritual journey is paramount to our success. Jesus had an insightful dialogue with His archenemies concerning this subject. Their exchange seems like an everyday conversation about the weather on the surface, but on further investigation it is incredibly profound. Let's jump into the middle of the conversation and see what we can learn.

> The Pharisees and Sadducees came up, and testing Jesus, they asked Him to show them a sign from heaven. But He replied to them, "When it is evening, you say, 'It will be fair weather, for the sky is red.' And in the morning, 'There will be a storm today, for the sky is red and threatening.' Do you know how to discern the appearance of the sky, but cannot discern the signs of the times?"

Matthew 16:1–3

The connotation is that the religious leaders understood how to predict the weather (a first-heaven manifestation of the elements), but they were blind to the divine *kairos* conditions (or divine opportune moments) wrought by the Kingdom of God. They were looking for Jesus to show them a sign from heaven, while the greatest sign from God in the history of the world was standing right in front of them, conversing with them!

Yet in a strange way, the Pharisees and Sadducees, although unable to "discern the signs of the times" for themselves, were aware that God creates kairos conditions that, like the weather, require preparation and dictate people's behavior. For instance, you probably are not going to plow your field when it looks as though it is about to rain. The religious leaders were keenly aware that God creates "signs" that clearly communicate kairos circumstances dictating the attitudes, mindsets and actions necessary to navigate His sovereign seasons successfully. Yet in this case, their "discerner" was broken. They were ships without a compass, trying desperately to navigate the seas of humanity without the benefit of the gear necessary to sail in security.

Unlike in Jesus' day, it is uncommon now to find any spiritual leader, or any follower of Jesus for that matter, who understands that there is such a thing as kairos times in the Spirit. Nor do they know how to navigate the planning and preparation for such times successfully.

Understanding the Times

In the Old Testament, there was a tribe of men called the sons of Issachar who were famous for understanding the "times," with knowledge of what Israel should do in those times (see 1 Chronicles 12:32). Before we go on, let me clarify what the Bible means by "times." The ancient Greeks had two words for time—*chronos* and *kairos*. The Greek word *chronos* is where we get our English word *chronological*, referring to a clock or calendar. *Chronos* is used 54 times in the New Testament, and it is time that can be measured in seconds, minutes, hours and years.

For instance, if I stepped into an elevator and asked you what time it is, you would probably look at your watch and report the "chronological" time of day. But the Issachar tribe was not famous for knowing the *chronos*; they were renowned for "understanding" the *kairos*. (Note that the Old Testament is written in Hebrew, and like our English language, Hebrew only has one word for time—*eth*. So in this case, we can only determine the definition of "the times" in the 1 Chronicles 12:32 passage by contextualizing the verse.)

The Greek word *kairos* is used 86 times in the New Testament, and it is qualitative. It measures moments, the right moment, the opportune moment, the perfect moment. It is important to know that the Greek word *kairos* in itself does not mean a divine time; it only describes a difference in the way we view time. But there are Kingdom kairos epochs that are predicated by a God-theme. These are kairos moments with a divine purpose and a presupposed outcome. (I will give you some examples of such moments in the list that follows.)

Such kairos times happen when divine favor meets divine opportunity. They are often the result of the sovereignty of God transcending the free will of man. The sons of Issachar were kairos conductors who, because they understood the times, were able to discern the appropriate action, act and/or attitude necessary to find synergy in these divine seasons.

Three things often mark divine kairos epochs: *acceleration*, *unusual occurrences* and *supernatural interventions*. Let's look at each of these more closely.

1. *Acceleration*—things that would normally take years happen suddenly. A great illustration of kairos acceleration took place in the rebuilding of the walls around Jerusalem, recounted in the book of Nehemiah. The walls were torn down for 114 years, and the Jews tried to rebuild them for 72 years. But what the Jews could not do in 72 years, Nehemiah did in 52 days. Furthermore, he accomplished this seemingly

impossible task with the same people who had failed for 72 years (see Nehemiah 1–6).

2. *Unusual occurrences*—things happen that seem outside the nature of God or unusual for the epoch season. The story of the death of Ananias and Sapphira is a perfect example of an unusual divine kairos occurrence in the early Church. The couple lied to the apostles about the price they had sold a piece of land for, and immediately God took their lives (see Acts 5:1–11). God transcended His New Covenant grace and mercy, including the message of loving His enemies, and instead made an executive decision to take their lives.

3. *Supernatural interventions*—things that never happen suddenly occur against ridiculous odds. One of the best illustrations of this is the wild story of Joshua pursuing the Amorites in battle. The momentum of the battle had shifted in Joshua's favor, but it was getting dark and he needed more time to crush his enemy. So he called out to the Lord and asked Him to cause the sun and moon to stand still, and they did! Ultimately, the extra light gave Joshua the advantage he needed to win the battle (see Joshua 10:12–13).

The Transition from Chronos to Kairos

We live day in and day out in chronos conditions, watching the clock and planning around our calendar. Then, sometimes without warning, we get drawn into the vortex of eternity and experience the effects of infinity. These are the divine kairos times in history when God overrides our free will and creates a supernatural exception to the rule. He defies the laws of physics or interrupts the trajectory of natural history to impose His sovereign will over humankind.

The truth is that God created us to be freewill agents. For example, God desires that everyone would go to heaven. Metaphorically speaking, Jesus basically said, "Over My dead body will you go to hell." But the truth is that there are people who will step over His "dead" body and choose hell over heaven.

"So why does God give people a free will?" you ask. Because love requires choice. It isn't instinctive and it can't be programmed into our DNA, because love is always an act of our will. God is therefore in charge, but He is not in control, so to speak. If God were controlling everything, there would be no such thing as murderers, rapists, child abductors, torturers or terrorists, but there would also be no *lovers*.

History is primarily molded by the will of people—until it isn't. What I mean is that there are moments in time when God interrupts history and creates *His-story*. This is where the vortex in the narrative of history changes. Free will gives way to sovereignty, and chronos yields to divine kairos moments. The challenge is that if we are spiritually ignorant and are unaware of the "change in weather" (which I call divine kairos conditions), then we can end up like Balaam, who demonstrated that a smart jackass is better than a dumb prophet!

King Balak wanted to hire Balaam the prophet to curse the Israelites so he could wipe them out. Balaam, riding his donkey on the road to his demise, suddenly encountered an angel of the Lord with sword drawn, ready to kill him (see Numbers 22:21–35). The dumb prophet was so spiritually blind that he did not even see the angel, but his donkey saw him and refused to go forward. Balaam beat the jackass three times, until the animal defiantly lay down.

> The LORD opened the mouth of the donkey, and she said to Balaam, "What have I done to you, that you have struck me these three times? ... Am I not your donkey on which you have ridden all your life to this day? Have I ever been accustomed to do so to you?"
>
> verses 28–30

Balaam answered no, and abruptly the Lord opened his eyes and he saw the angel in front of him, ready to kill him with his sword. This story proves that even a jackass can receive spiritual insights. Yet more importantly, this crazy fable warns us of the destructive nature of arrogance and selfish ambition. It demonstrates that virtueless attributes can blind us to third-heaven realities, which ultimately interferes with our God-given purpose.

I have to admit that years ago I had a similar experience, although it lacked the talking jackass. At the time, I was going through a very difficult season in my life. Much like Joseph in the Old Testament, who had received a word from God that he would become a great world leader, yet found himself living as a slave in Egypt, I, too, was living a life opposite of my prophetic purpose. One day, I decided I would reverse course and do my own thing. Then suddenly, I had a vision of God walking very intentionally down a path. People were standing in front of Him, trying to deter His progress, as if they were defensive linemen in a football game. God grabbed them and threw them left and right, as if they were rag dolls.

Then the scene changed, and I was the next one in front of God, looking as if I were going to try to block His progress. He looked me right in the eyes and shouted, *Get out of My way!* Next, He reached out to grab my arm just as I moved aside in time to let Him pass. As He passed by me, He never turned around, but I heard Him yell, *Now follow Me!*

The truth is that God is often moving in our lives at a speed that is creating divine kairos conditions. This creates an urgency for us to step out of the way of what He is doing and follow Him. In these divine kairos conditions, God takes history out of the hands of people and molds and shapes it as a potter works the clay.

I have observed many people over the years who were unaware of the significance of their divine kairos moments. Much like Ananias and Sapphira, who were caught snoozing at their wheel of fortune and ran their ship aground on the shore of devastation, these people also crash and burn. People have lied for years without negative repercussions. In fact, Ananias and Sapphira were being questioned by the most famous liar in the Bible—Peter. Three times, he lied about knowing the Lord. So it's not just that Ananias and Sapphira lied; it's *when* they lied that created such a harsh reality for them. So I rarely use their example in my teaching, because my primary concern has always been that we would then create a culture out of an exception by misunderstanding the difference between a divine kairos act of sovereignty and the grace-filled gravity of everyday free will in Jesus. Yet the fear of the Lord compels me to teach the people of God about sovereign moments and the heightened respect that is necessary to navigate these divine kairos seasons with the wisdom of the ageless One.

Changing Songs

Somewhere around three thousand years ago, the prophet Isaiah made a powerful declaration concerning the transitioning of epoch seasons. He declared,

> "Behold, the former things have come to pass,
> Now I declare new things;
> Before they spring forth I proclaim them to you."
>
> Sing to the LORD a new song,
> Sing His praise from the end of the earth!
>
> Isaiah 42:9–10

The prophet Isaiah is famous for using language with double meanings and/or pictorial metaphors to express his point. Here, Isaiah describes the close of one season and the opening of another, and then finishes his exhortation with a command to sing a "new song" to the Lord. There are several profound insights here that I want to unearth with you. The first is that Isaiah said God is doing a "new" thing, not the next thing! If God were doing the next thing, then the former thing would have something to do with our next season. But instead, God is doing a whole new thing.

Second, the "new" thing will require us to sing a "new song." I am certain that this verse has a double meaning, in which the prophet is pointing out that a "new song" (meaning a new way of thinking) is necessary for a "new season." Additionally, he explains that this new song needs to be sung to the Lord. This means that this new season will inspire a higher level of revelation concerning the nature of God's character.

"How do you know that the revelation is about God's nature?" you ask. Because the prophet says, "Sing His *praise* from the end of the earth!" Unlike thanksgiving, which is our response to God's works or actions in our lives, praise is our response to His nature or character.

Furthermore, we will sing to the "end of the earth," meaning the new thing will have global impact. And finally, Isaiah is proclaiming it *before* it happens. This indicates that God is calling things that *are not* as though *they are*, which is catalyzing the cosmos into divine order for the coming epoch era.

Let's dig a little deeper to inspire us to a higher level of spiritual intelligence. Jesus also used "songs" to depict changing kairos seasons when He said,

> To what then shall I compare the men of this generation, and what are they like? They are like children who sit in the market place and call to one another, and they say, "We played the flute for you, and you did not dance; we sang a dirge, and you did not weep." For John the Baptist has come eating no bread and drinking no wine, and you say, "He has a demon!" The Son of Man has come eating and drinking, and you say, "Behold, a gluttonous man and a drunkard, a friend of tax collectors and sinners!" Yet wisdom is vindicated by all her children.

Luke 7:31–35

Jesus said that John the Baptist sang the "dirge" (by fasting). The dirge is a song sung at funerals. He goes on to indicate that He

Himself played the flute (by feasting), which was the instrument used in weddings. But the religious leaders of the day were offended by the vessels that carried the message, namely John and Jesus. Consequently, they didn't behave appropriately under those divine kairos conditions. They didn't mourn when it was time to mourn, and they didn't dance when it was time to celebrate.

Writer and futurist Alvin Toffler made a profound statement that I think applies not only to the religious leaders of Jesus' day, but is also a powerful warning for us all: "The illiterate of the future will not be the person who cannot read. It will be the person who does not know how to learn." The spiritual leaders of Jesus' day were so steeped in religion, jealousy and offense that they literally forgot how to learn.

We must not become like them. It is imperative that we become spiritually intelligent believers who are allowing the Holy Spirit to lead us into all truth. To accomplish this, one of the first questions we have to answer is, *Do we actually know what time it is?* We have to press into the Spirit to discern the times, the divine kairos moments in our epoch history. Do we actually know what "song" is playing in our lives? Do we have the spiritual intelligence, expressed through the divine wisdom of the Spirit, to understand what the proper response is to our epoch season?

It is so important that we know when to dance and when to mourn. Solomon got it right in the book of Ecclesiastes when he described different kairos conditions:

There is an appointed time for everything. And there is a time for every event under heaven:

A time to give birth and a time to die;
A time to plant and a time to uproot what is planted.
A time to kill and a time to heal;
A time to tear down and a time to build up.
A time to weep and a time to laugh;

A time to mourn and a time to dance.

A time to throw stones and a time to gather stones;

A time to embrace and a time to shun embracing.

A time to search and a time to give up as lost;

A time to keep and a time to throw away.

A time to tear apart and a time to sew together;

A time to be silent and a time to speak.

A time to love and a time to hate.

A time for war and a time for peace. . . .

He has made everything appropriate in its time. He has also set eternity in their heart, yet so that man will not find out the work which God has done from the beginning even to the end.

Ecclesiastes 3:1–8, 11

Solomon is pointing out that there is actually a kairos time for everything that happens in life. Remember, the Greek word *kairos* is not used in the Old Testament, which was originally written in the Hebrew language. But Solomon's description in these passages is the definition of kairos times.

One of the saddest stories in the entire Bible took place when Solomon's father, David, the "man after God's heart," became incongruent with the kairos season of his life:

Then it happened in the spring, at the time when kings go out to battle, that David sent Joab and his servants with him and all Israel, and they destroyed the sons of Ammon and besieged Rabbah. But David stayed at Jerusalem.

Now when evening came David arose from his bed and walked around on the roof of the king's house, and from the roof he saw a woman bathing; and the woman was very beautiful in appearance. So David sent and inquired about the woman. And one said, "Is this not Bathsheba, the daughter of Eliam, the wife of Uriah the Hittite?" David sent messengers and took her, and when she came to him, he lay with her; and when she had purified herself from her uncleanness, she returned to her house. The woman conceived; and she sent and told David, and said, "I am pregnant."

2 Samuel 11:1–5

Did you notice that "at the time when kings go out to battle," David stayed at home? It was a time for war, but David acted as if it were a time for peace. David had many wives and concubines, so the mismanagement of his sex drive certainly wasn't the only issue here. Instead, he misjudged the kairos conditions of his life and fell into sin.

It is important to understand that the safest place on earth to be is in God's will, whether that is on the battlefield or in the palace parlor. The story goes on to tell us that David murdered Uriah, Bathsheba's husband, to cover up his own affair with her. Uriah was one of David's 33 mighty men, and his name means, "God is my fire." On that fateful day, the fire of God went out in King David's life. He never fully recovered from his fall with Bathsheba. God, however, remained faithful to David and caused his wife Bathsheba to become the mother of Solomon, the next great king of Israel.

Profound Kairos Shifts

The Bible gives us so many examples of sudden shifts in kairos conditions, moments in which God became the divine x factor to a "new thing." In the story of the Tower of Babel, the people decided to build a tower to heaven for themselves (see Genesis 11:1–9). They worked on the thing for years, until one day God showed up, checked out their work and said, "Behold, they are one people, and they all have the same language. And this is what they began to do, and now nothing which they purpose to do will be impossible for them" (verse 6). So He confused their language, and the work stopped because the people could not communicate with each other. It's kind of funny, really. One day you are doing fine, and the next day you are doing time!

Then there's the famous story of the Israelites being enslaved in Egypt for four hundred years, until God decided to send Moses to deliver them. Interestingly, Moses had tried to free the Israelites forty years earlier but had failed miserably. Moses was the right guy for the job, but he didn't "understand the times." Like the Pharisees and Sadducees of Jesus' day, Moses had not yet learned how to discern the kairos seasons of God's divine providence. God had spoken to Abraham hundreds of years before Moses and had said this:

> Know for certain that your descendants will be strangers in a land that is not theirs, where they will be enslaved and oppressed four hundred years. But I will also judge the nation whom they will serve, and afterward they will come out with many possessions.
>
> Genesis 15:13–14

God went on to say that He would deliver them and they would return when the "iniquity of the Amorites" was complete (verse 16).

Much like Moses, we often have a burning call in our lives to accomplish something significant for God, yet our first attempts frequently fail because we have yet to tap into SQ deeply enough to understand the kairos conditions necessary to be successful. Philosopher Eric Hoffer said, "In times of change, learners inherit the earth, while the learned find themselves beautifully equipped to deal with a world that no longer exists." It is imperative in kairos transitions that we remain teachable and hungry so that we learn and grow.

Sometimes the greatest challenge we have in a new season is that we know too much about our previous mandate. We are so familiar with the "old song" that we don't really want to hear the new music. That's why the greatest resisters of the "new thing" are people who succeeded in the "old thing." We become SQ midgets because we are IQ geniuses. We treat every season in life as if it is the "next thing," usually because we feel terribly disqualified and ill-equipped for a place that we have never been before. Then we wonder why we are bored to death and feel disconnected from the Spirit.

Anachronistic Living

When we settle into trusting the Spirit to guide our lives and we begin to plug into our prophetic gifts, we can sometimes find ourselves living *in* the future instead of *from* the future. We need to honor the past, live in the present and look to the future. One challenge for prophetic people is that as they get insights into the future, they often begin to live there before it is actually available to them. Again, Moses is a great example of a man who had a deep sense of his future call, but a terrible sense of prophetic timing.

My good friend Dano McCollam said this about spiritually intelligent people:

> Often the prophetic dream, revelation, oracle or vision is a greater reality to the prophetic person than current events. The prophetic person must make a commitment to learn how to live out of time. This is anachronistic living. Anachronism is defined as *anything out of its proper time. It's the representation of something as existing or happening at other than its proper or historical time.*

I would like to revisit the prophet Habakkuk's declaration that clarifies the nature of the prophetic promise. He wrote, "For the vision is yet for the appointed time; it hastens toward the goal and it will not fail. Though it tarries, wait for it; for it will certainly come, it will not delay" (Habakkuk 2:3). We must contend for the promise that tarries. The Hebrew word *tarries* means "to question, to hesitate, to be reluctant, delay, or linger." There are many times that a prophetic promise seems to take forever to be fulfilled. Remember, it took eighty years in the life of Moses. Yet we are instructed to "wait for it." The Hebrew word *wait* means "to be entrenched," or "to dig deep."

In other words, prepare yourself for the long hall (and haul). I love the humorous way pastor and teacher Joseph Garlington described seasons of transition. He said, "God opens one door and closes another, but it's hell in the hallway!"

15

Finding Missing Children

Speaking of kairos conditions, it is high time for us to unseat the psychics who have stolen our God-appointed seats among the kings of the earth. They have somehow managed to creep into nearly every realm of society with their twisted second-heaven insights, and have manipulated the epoch situations. From the White House to the outhouse and everything in between, psychics are guiding society to the sheer cliff of a disastrous demise. Cloaked within a sense of decency, they are luring kings away from the pure counsel of the Lord. It is high time that we emerge, like Daniel and the three boys in Babylon, and challenge their second-heaven perceptions with third-heaven insights and supernatural wisdom.

"Where do we start?" you query. We begin by tapping into our spiritual gifts in everyday life situations. As we prove ourselves faithful stewards of our divine abilities, God expands our capacity and increases the size and scope of our spheres of influence. Faithfulness is the pathway to promotion in the Spirit.

Let me share another piece of my journey with you that demonstrates how God has opened up opportunities for me to grow in my supernatural abilities. In October 2001, Kathy and I got a call on a Saturday afternoon from our close friend Sheri Silk. In a panic, Sheri began to recount her teenage daughter's perilous situation: "We just found out that Brittney has been having an online relationship with some kid! This morning she disappeared, and we can't find her. She isn't answering her phone! Please pray," she exhorted.

"Don't worry. We'll find her," we reassured Sheri.

We hung up the phone and began to pray right there in the kitchen. Sheri had mentioned that Brittney's cousin said she was at a park, but there are countless parks in Redding, so the chances of finding her at a random park were slim. As we prayed, a vision emerged in my mind of Brittney's car parked at a trailhead. I described the vision to Kathy in detail. I saw a gravel parking lot, and the river was on the right side of the lot, which was just off the shoulder of a road, close to a bridge.

Kathy blurted out, "I know exactly where that is!" We jumped in our car and headed to the trailhead, while Kathy called Sheri back and explained the situation.

A few minutes later, we pulled up at the trailhead I had envisioned (inside a park), and sure enough, Brittney was standing next to her car with a young man. I called out to her, and she came over and talked to Kathy.

I walked over and had a conversation with the boy. The kid was terrified as he tried to explain, "Sorry, mister! I was trying to see my . . . I just wanted to talk to my . . . friend. I didn't mean to do it, sir . . . man!"

In the meantime, Kathy handed the phone to Brittney, who briefly talked to her dad. Kathy then drove Brittney home in her car, while I followed them in ours. We chatted with the Silks for a few minutes and then left so they could talk as a family. Thankfully, this particular story has a beautiful ending. You can read about it in more detail in Danny Silk's book *Loving Our Kids on Purpose* (Destiny Image, 2016).

Divine Possibilities

It is funny how often God uses the challenges of our lives to inspire divine opportunities and open our spirits to new possibilities. After the situation with Brittney, I began to dream of using SQ to find missing children. I wondered what it would be like to build a relationship with the police or FBI to help find the 800,000 kids who go missing every year.

My close friend Dano McCollam, whom I have already mentioned, is a prophet I have known for twenty years. The two of us developed a weeklong "School of the Prophets" training event that we have held every year for more than fourteen years. The goal of the school is to teach people how to develop their spiritual intelligence and how to use the gift to improve the state of the earth.

One day around the Christmas season, Dano was doing some research on Saint Nicholas. (That's right—Santa Claus was a real person.) Dano discovered that Nicholas was a "patron saint of children" because of his acts of generosity to the poor. There were also many powerful accounts of Saint Nick using SQ to rescue kidnapped children, especially the gift of the word of knowledge. It is reported that Saint Nick singlehandedly broke up the child slavery rings of his day.

Dano was so inspired by the life of Nicholas that he longed to do the same thing. One day while praying about this idea, a vision appeared to him. He suddenly saw in his spirit pictures of missing children that line the exits of our large American department stores. As the vision grew in his mind, a deep burden emerged in his heart to help the parents of these kids find them.

The Great Experiment

Dano became plagued with this passion to pick up Saint Nick's torch (although thankfully not the Santa Claus role), so he made a decision to go after this kind of spiritual intelligence in his own prophetic community. He hosts a monthly gathering of people who have highly developed SQ. He calls them his "Prophetic Company." Dano decided to experiment with them by printing posters he found on the Internet of missing children from his area. The posters had the backstory and the details of each child's abduction. Then he divided his Prophetic Company into ten teams of eight members and gave each team a poster.

Prophetic coaches were assigned to each group to facilitate the teams. The coaches had a printout of the details and/or backstory of the abduction, but they were instructed to keep the information to themselves. The only clues the team members were given were the name and picture of the child.

"Radical!" you say? Yes, but wait, this gets really good! Next, each team member tapped into his or her SQ to get any information he or she could with regard to the child's abduction. The coaches then checked the accuracy of the team's perceptions against the backstory they had been provided along with the child's poster.

The idea was that if the information coming from a word of knowledge was on track, then they knew they heard clearly from the Lord, which created confidence to dig deeper into the abduction. The members of the Prophetic Company worked independently within their groups to get information and perceptions from the Lord. Then they would all come together and share their impressions. Whenever two or more of the team members had the same impression or information, that revelation took on a higher priority.

One of the first abductions the Prophetic Company took on was a little girl. They became passionate about finding her. Then suddenly in one of the practice exercises, a team member accurately perceived the names of the two suspects involved, as well as the make, model and color of the car used to abduct the child. The missing children's website allowed the team to verify parts of these facts, and the precision of this word of knowledge caused their faith to soar. They knew by the Spirit that the little girl was still alive, so they pressed in for more clarity. God gave them pictures and perceptions of where the child was being held, along with His wisdom on how she could escape or be rescued. The company then began to pray and declare her freedom into the spiritual atmosphere. A few days later, the little girl (who had been missing for more than a year) was found and miraculously restored to her family. Now that rocks!

This opened a door into the local police department. The police officers were so impressed with this prophetic process and divine accuracy that they began to invite the Prophetic Company to use their SQ to press in for information regarding other missing children from the local caseload, one of whom had special needs that made it greatly urgent that the child be found.

Immediately, a member of the company received three clues from the Lord. She saw a house of a particular color, on a street that began with a specific letter, and she recognized it as the house of someone whom the child knew. Those clues resulted in a police officer finding the missing child within 24 hours—in a house that matched all three clues.

The Prophetic Company then was invited to partner with the police department to find missing children and help solve unsolved crimes. A local police officer was brought in who trained the teams in how to communicate with law enforcement agencies and how to understand their specific protocols. As word spread about the team's success, various requests for help came in from police, family members, the FBI and private investigators. The Prophetic Company literally helped solve a number of crimes, and also assisted in finding many missing children.

Today, Dano's Prophetic Company has an online partnership with over four thousand "prophetic finder" volunteers. These prophetic teams have tapped into their SQ to help solve crimes and find missing persons all over the world. Many of their partners have become much more skilled and accurate than the original team members, and consequently several of them are serving at the highest levels of government within their nations.

You're Next

Dano and his team are forging a new era of supernatural people who are literally rewriting the history of the nations. He has become a modern-day Daniel working with the kings of our day.

The Magi were stargazers who brought gifts to Jesus at His birth. Their lineage is traced all the way back to Daniel in Babylon. In fact, the Magi who brought gifts to the Messiah were the spiritual grandsons of the prophet Daniel, who became chief of the magicians in the days of King Nebuchadnezzar. Daniel unseated the sorcerers of his day, as he was ten times wiser than all of them. Furthermore, he became the mentor of many of the magicians who turned to Jehovah from demons and idols.

History is repeating itself as God is again moving among His people with supernatural power and divine wisdom. In a few short years, every police station in the world will be tapping into spiritual intelligence through God's powerful people. You might be next! Prepare yourself for the "new thing" God is doing in the earth and in you.

16

AirDrop Spirit to Spirit

An incredible dynamic takes place in us as believers as a result of the Holy Spirit simultaneously living in us individually and collectively. The Bible explains this dynamic 1 Corinthians 12:1–11, which is often misunderstood or taught incorrectly. Let's look at it together:

> Now concerning spiritual *gifts*, brethren, I do not want you to be unaware. You know that when you were pagans, you were led astray to the mute idols, however you were led. . . .
>
> Now there are varieties of gifts, but the *same* Spirit. And there are varieties of ministries, and the *same* Lord. There are varieties of effects, but the *same* God who works all things in all persons. But to each one is given the manifestation of the Spirit for the common good. For to one is given the word of wisdom through the Spirit, and to another the word of knowledge according to the *same* Spirit; to another faith by the *same* Spirit, and to another gifts of healing by the *one* Spirit, and to another the effecting of miracles, and to another prophecy, and to another the distinguishing of spirits, to another various kinds of tongues, and to another the interpretation

of tongues. But one and the *same* Spirit works all these things, distributing to each one individually just as He wills.

In the version I quoted (NASB, emphasis added), the word *gifts* is italicized in the first verse because it is not in the original Greek text. The verse should read, "Now concerning the *spiritual*, brethren, I don't want you to be unaware." The apostle Paul's intention was to teach the Corinthians, who were former polytheists (meaning they believed in multiple gods), how the spirit world actually works.

Now read the rest of the passage carefully. Did you catch the operative word in the text? I also italicized the common operative word, *same*, so you would catch it. Why does Paul keep using the word *same*—*same* Spirit, *same* Lord, *same* God? He is using the word *same* to correct the Greek idea that each gift of the Spirit is a different god. The Corinthians were moving in the gifts of the Holy Spirit, but they had superimposed their doctrine of polytheism over their experience. They were having the right experience, but holding to the wrong theology. Paul is pointing out that the person who is ministering in the gift of prophecy has the *same* Spirit as the person who is getting someone well with the gift of healing in the same moment, and so forth.

The Greeks could not envision a God who lives outside the laws of physics, and who is omnipresent everywhere at once, working through different gifts and various people all at the same time. The truth is that God could be having an intimate conversation with you while He is correcting me, rejoicing with someone who just got saved, and being angry with a murderer who took the life of someone—all at the same time! God can have a personal relationship with 7.7 billion people on the planet, carry on a conversation with all of them at the same time and still have the bandwidth to create another universe . . . all simultaneously. God is not human; He is *God*.

The Spiritual Internet

Remember that back in chapter 1, I talked about how smartphones are limited to their own stored memory, yet they can also access the Internet, which has billions of times more information than what could ever be stored on one smartphone's memory? With that in mind, think about this: What if you could connect with other people's "hard drives" and stored memories? Or if not with their memories, at least with the benefit of their positive outcomes? What if the things you gained in God over your lifetime could be transferred to other people's spiritual accounts? This is possible, and it is the apex of spiritual inheritance.

The fact that God is in all of us at once creates a sort of spiritual Internet by which we can both access collective intelligence and "AirDrop" spiritual gifts to one another. Let me explain it like this: If the same Spirit is in you and in me concurrently, then we actually have a spiritual connection in that our *human* spirits are in union with one another through the conduit of the Holy Spirit. Whatever I gain in the Spirit, I can therefore pass to you through the Holy Spirit whom we both share. Here is an example of Paul reminding his disciple Timothy of the AirDrop that took place in his spirit:

> Do not neglect the spiritual gift within you, which was bestowed on you through prophetic utterance with the laying on of hands by the presbytery. Take pains with these things; be absorbed in them, so that your progress will be evident to all.
>
> 1 Timothy 4:14–15

These verses describe in great detail the way this spiritual AirDrop took place. Paul said that a group of leaders (called the presbytery) laid their hands on Timothy. While prophesying, the transfer of the gift was moving from their spirits to his spirit. Paul went on to exhort Tim to grow the gift given to him through intense labor so that everyone around him could observe his forward progress in the supernatural ability imparted to him from them.

Paul described several of the Holy Spirit's *gifts, ministries* and *effects* in 1 Corinthians 12:1–11. A variety of manifestations is supernaturally activated through the Holy Spirit's impartation. The word *ministry* in that passage is the Greek word *diakonia*, which means "spiritual occupations." This could refer to a teacher, pastor, evangelist and so forth.

The word *effect* is the Greek word *energeo*. It means "spiritual accomplishments," as in work achieved or performed by the Holy Spirit, such as when a person is saved by the direction of the Spirit, or when the Spirit flowing through a believer heals a marriage.

The word *gifts* is the Greek word *charisma*, and in this passage it means "spiritual abilities." These are all actually different dimensions of spiritual intelligence and supernatural power. Here is a brief overview of a few of the gifts of the Spirit and their definitions:

1. The gift of discernment/distinguishing of spirits (1 Corinthians 12:10)

   The ability to accurately perceive spiritual entities that are influencing people, organizations and geographic locations, and that are affecting people's motivations, attitudes, inclinations and mindsets

   The ability to appraise the level of spiritual favor and the strength of the human spirit that is present in the triune being of each individual

2. The gift of knowledge (1 Corinthians 12:8)

   The ability to receive facts and pertinent information about the visible dimension/world by communicating with the Holy Spirit

3. The gift of wisdom (1 Corinthians 12:8)

   The ability to rightly apply knowledge in a way that builds for the future that which was envisioned by the

Creator, so that we develop a divine ecosystem that will yield life

4. The gift of prophecy (1 Corinthians 12:10)

The ability to foresee the future before it happens

The ability to understand a person, organization and/or geographic location's divine purpose and call

The ability to call things that are not as though they are and thus "procreate" with God in the sense of partnering creatively (see Romans 4:17); this is the forthtelling dimension of the gift of prophecy

5. The mind of Christ (1 Corinthians 2:6–16)

The ability to process all aspects of life from an eternal, timeless and multidimensional perspective

The ability to think supernaturally and perceive the natural world through infinite probabilities and limitless resources that transcend the laws of physics and the restrictions of physical realities

These are just a few of the gifts and abilities manifested through spiritual intelligence. But it is important to remember that the same gifts can manifest differently through various ministries and also have different effects in diverse environments. For example, the word of knowledge can be used to diagnose a health issue in a person's life or to troubleshoot an automobile's problem through an automotive technician's ministry.

There is another manifestation of spiritual intelligence that I call "collective reasoning." The apostle Paul wrote that "we have the mind of Christ" (1 Corinthians 2:16). Notice how he says that "we" have the mind of Christ, not individually, but collectively. Spiritual collective intelligence is not the sum total SQ of the people in a room, but is a manifestation of the Spirit flowing in harmony through individual members of the Body of Christ (see Romans 12:4). Paul put it best, saying that we ought to be "diligent to preserve the unity of the Spirit in the bond of peace" (Ephesians 4:3). It is apparent that the main catalyst for collective intelligence is inspired by each of us "preserving the unity of the Spirit" by loving one another practically and passionately.

There is also a dimension of spiritual intelligence that is profound but often overlooked. It is personified in this verse: "For I am mindful of the sincere faith within you [Timothy], which first dwelt in your grandmother Lois and your mother Eunice, and I am sure that it is in you as well" (2 Timothy 1:5). The Bible strongly implies here that Timothy's faith was the result of a spiritual inheritance from his grandmother and mother. The spirit world transcends time and space. When someone wins a personal victory with God, it therefore becomes a spiritual inheritance to those who come after that person in the Spirit.

Let me be clear, however, that just because your parents or grandparents were spiritual giants does not mean you will tap into their inheritance. The inheritance passes from Spirit to spirit; thus a person who does not walk with Christ and is void of the Spirit does not have the eternal equipment necessary to "AirDrop" their inheritance.

The Advantages of God's Superheroes

Let's summarize the incredible advantages of God's superheroes, who are believers who know their God and do great exploits. Jesus made this profound statement: "Truly I say to you, among those born of women there has not arisen anyone greater than John the Baptist! Yet the one who is least in the kingdom of heaven is greater than he" (Matthew 11:11). John the Baptist was the greatest prophet of the entire Old Covenant, yet the least (the weakest saint in the Kingdom) is greater than John.

"What did you just say?" you ask. First of all, I didn't say it; I was quoting Jesus. He said it. Many of the Old Testament believers were world changers! I mean, wouldn't you love for your name even to be whispered among those in the hall of faith—saints like Abraham, Sarah, Moses, Joshua or even King David, the man after God's heart? Or how about the great prophets Elijah, Elisha and Deborah, men and women who literally shifted the course of nations? Yet the truth is that if you are a born-again believer, you have an incredible advantage over any of the Old Testament saints.

The Old Testament was the dispensation before the death and resurrection of Christ. When Jesus died on the cross, Scripture says that we died with Him, and that when He rose again, we rose with Him (see Romans 6). It also says, "Therefore if anyone is in Christ, he is a new creature; the old things passed away; behold, new things have come" (2 Corinthians 5:17). The word *new* here is the Greek word *kainos*, which can be translated as "prototype"—something never before created. When we received Christ, we became creatures who had never before graced this planet. Consequently, the blood of Jesus didn't just cleanse us from all sin; it transformed us into the likeness of Christ. In fact, the Bible says, "Therefore be imitators of God, as beloved children" (Ephesians 5:1) The goal of discipleship is to become like God.

I know, I know, you might be freaking out by now, saying, "We aren't supposed to be like God; we are supposed to be Christlike!" Let's think about that for a minute. Jesus is God, so becoming Christlike is becoming like God. Now, I'm not talking about becoming a god! I'm simply pointing out that we were created in the image and likeness of God, and He is our heavenly Father. So it is natural for us to be like our Daddy.

How are you doing at thinking the way your Father does? In other words, are you applying your spiritual intelligence to a world greatly in need of His wisdom and heaven-inspired solutions? As you finish reading this final chapter, don't forget to take the *Spiritual Intelligence Quotient (SQ) Assessment* I have included at the end of the book (if you haven't taken it already). As I said earlier, it will help you assess your current level of SQ and also increase it. Once you know your SQ scores, there are specific action steps you can take to help you begin thinking in new and supernatural ways—like your Father—that will benefit the people and the world around you.

Furthermore, God empowered us to do greater works than Christ did, so we can ascertain that being Christlike is more than having a noble character; it is also operating in divine power. Here is a summary of twenty ways New Testament believers are more supernaturally equipped than either unbelievers or our Old Testament counterparts. (I have mentioned many of these already throughout the book, but this list serves as a powerful reminder.)

1. We are born-again believers, which means we have a new heart and a new mind (see Ezekiel 36:26; 1 Corinthians 2:16). Old Testament believers had a sin nature, but we are saints, meaning "holy believers." Non-Christians are slaves to sin, as we all once were, but believers can be free from sin (see Romans 6:6).

2. We are seated in heavenly places with Christ. Our heavenly seat gives us eternal perspectives (see Ephesians 2:6; Revelation 4:1), whereas non-Christians are relegated only to the first heaven.

3. The Creator Himself actually lives inside us (see 1 Corinthians 3:16). In the Old Testament, the Spirit came *on* people, but in the New Testament, He lives *in* us.

4. Jesus said, "No longer do I call you slaves, for the slave does not know what his master is doing; but I have called you friends, for all things that I have heard from My Father I have made known to you" (John 15:15). Friendship with God releases divine revelation in us. We therefore can know all things, as the Spirit reveals them. Unbelievers are consigned only to IQ and EQ.

5. We have angelic insights and angel oversight (see Acts 10:3–7; Hebrews 1:5–14).

6. We have been enlightened as believers (see Hebrews 6:4).

7. We have access to the powers of the age to come (see Hebrews 6:5).

8. "We are His workmanship, created in Christ Jesus for good works, which God prepared beforehand so that we would walk in them" (Ephesians 2:10). God prepared our work before He created us in Christ, so our divine advantage is that we can't fail, because He designed us for our mission. This is all "in Christ," meaning that those without Christ have yet to experience this divine benefit.

9. We have been given authority and power over all the power of the evil one (see Luke 9:1). Pre-Christians are under the power and influence of the devil (see Ephesians 2:1–2).

10. We have been given all *authority* to make disciples of all nations (see Matthew 28:18–20). Believers are specifically called to lead nations and be cultural architects.

11. We have at least five dimensions of wisdom, the first of which is that we have the Holy Spirit's gift of wisdom (see 1 Corinthians 12:8).

12. The second dimension is that we have the wisdom rooted in the mind of Christ (see 1 Corinthians 2:16).

13. The third dimension is that we have the timeless wisdom founded in eternity, called "the wisdom from the age to come" (see 1 Corinthians 2:6–7).

14. The fourth dimension is that we have the "manifold wisdom of God," which is multidimensional (see Ephesians 3:10).

15. The fifth dimension is that we have the collective wisdom rooted in impartation and cooperative reasoning (see Romans 1:11).

16. We have the gift of prophecy, which is foretelling, or the ability to know the future before it happens. It is also forthtelling, which is causing the future with God's prophetic insights (see 1 Corinthians 12:10; Ezekiel 37:1–10).

17. We have the gift of discernment, which helps us navigate the unseen realm holistically (see 1 Corinthians 12:10; 1 John 4:1–4).

18. We have the Holy Spirit in us, who guides us into *all* truth (see John 16:13).

19. We have the Spirit of revelation resting on us, which gives us insights into the Word of God (see Ephesians 1:17).

20. We have the gift of the word of knowledge, by which we know facts through the insights of the Holy Spirit (see 1 Corinthians 12:8).

Why the Discrepancy?

The million-dollar question is, If these things are true about believers, then why aren't we leading every realm of society? Why is it that the most creative, innovative, inventive, intelligent and gifted leaders in the world often aren't Christians? I think it is because the wisdom we get from God is imprisoned in us as believers, guarded by the spirit of religion, shackled for generations by the fear of man, and locked away by mediocrity that undermines excellence and kills inspiration.

Jesus warned us about this spirit of religion. He said, "Beware of the leaven of the Pharisees and Sadducees" (Matthew 16:6). Furthermore, the political spirit has robbed us of the mind of Christ by disarming creativity and marching Christian soldiers to the concentration camp of black-and-white thinking. This accumulative demise has often reduced the most brilliant people on the planet to an echo rather than a voice.

We have mirrored worldly thinking, which has undermined the triumphant call on us to rise and shine with ageless wisdom and supernatural power. Jesus also cautioned us about this political spirit when He said that in addition to the leaven of the Pharisees, we should beware of "the leaven of Herod" (Mark 8:15).

The Coming Reformation

Amid this devilish demise, there is an ancient promise of profound proportions that reverberates from an old prophet who peered into the future and spoke of a kairos shift in the condition of the earth. Isaiah proclaimed,

> Arise, shine; for your light has come, and the glory of the LORD has risen upon you. For behold, darkness will cover the earth and deep darkness the peoples; but the LORD will rise upon you and His glory will appear upon you. Nations will come to your light, and kings to the brightness of your rising.
>
> Isaiah 60:1–3

The conditions of this rising are familiar to us all. "Deep darkness" is the hopeless depression and moral decay entrenched in the nations. Yet against the backdrop of this darkness, God's people are rising with divine favor and supernatural insights. Jesus authenticated this prophetic declaration when He announced, "You are the light of the world. A city set on a hill cannot be hidden" (Matthew 5:14). Look at the profound response to this epic rising:

> Lift up your eyes round about and see; they all gather together, they come to you. Your sons will come from afar, and your daughters will be carried in the arms. Then you will see and be radiant, and your heart will thrill and rejoice; because the abundance of the sea will be turned to you, the wealth of the nations will come to you.
>
> Isaiah 60:4–5

The divine light, which inspires revelation, insights and supernatural solutions, attracts the world like moths to a lamp, forging a *High*-way for the restoration of communities and families. The prophet Malachi mirrored this declaration just four hundred years before Christ, writing, "Behold, I am going to send you Elijah the prophet before the coming of the great and terrible day of the LORD. He will restore the hearts of the fathers to their children and the hearts of the children to their fathers" (Malachi 4:5–6).

A divine shift is taking place in the Spirit, and it is having great impact on humankind. Like the instinctive nature in birds that migrate south in the winter, people are experiencing a spiritual awakening and are making the voyage back to their Creator, Lover and Friend. Isaiah went on to proclaim, "Your gates will be open continually; they will not be closed day or night, so that men may bring to you the wealth of the nations, with their kings led in procession" (Isaiah 60:11).

These kairos conditions echo the days of King Solomon, when God put His divine wisdom on display for all the known world through the king of Israel. Literally, kings and queens came from around the world to experience Solomon's wisdom. Here is a short excerpt from the queen of Sheba that highlights the nature of Solomon's wisdom:

> When the queen of Sheba perceived all the wisdom of Solomon, the house that he had built, the food of his table, the seating of his servants, the attendance of his waiters and their attire, his cupbearers, and his stairway by which he went up to the house of the LORD, there was no more spirit in her. Then she said to the king, "It was a true report which I heard in my own land about your words and your wisdom. Nevertheless I did not believe the reports, until I came and my eyes had seen it. And behold, the half was not told me. You exceed in wisdom and prosperity the report which I heard."
>
> 1 Kings 10:4–7

The queen was so rocked by Solomon's brilliant wisdom that she gave him a huge offering and said this:

> "Blessed be the LORD your God who delighted in you to set you on the throne of Israel; because the LORD loved Israel forever, therefore He made you king, to do justice and righteousness." She gave the king a hundred and twenty talents of gold, and a very great amount of spices and precious stones. Never again did such abundance of spices come in as that which the queen of Sheba gave King Solomon.
>
> 1 Kings 10:9–10

I think it is important to note that Solomon monetized his intellectual property three thousand years before there was an Information Age, and long before Apple, Google, Microsoft or even the invention of the microchip ever existed. The queen of Sheba did not hear Solomon spouting off some cool-sounding philosophies. Instead, she experienced God's wisdom that created a superior ecosystem, which looked practical on the outside but was centered in God's divine providence. That rich lady emptied her treasures and dumped a heap on a guy who downloaded heaven on her.

Cloud Cover

This is a great story, but how about us? How are we going to respond? If you have forged your way this far into the depths of this manuscript, then it is critical for you to understand that we are being stalked. That's right! Moreover, our history is being uploaded to *"the Cloud"* through a family of watching waiters who are chronicling our profound narrative. The author of Hebrews uncovered this divine dynamic:

> Therefore, since we have so great a cloud of witnesses surrounding us, let us also lay aside every encumbrance and the sin which so easily

entangles us, and let us run with endurance the race that is set before us, fixing our eyes on Jesus, the author and perfecter of faith, who for the joy set before Him endured the cross, despising the shame, and has sat down at the right hand of the throne of God.

Hebrews 12:1–2

The Greek word *cloud* in this passage is *nephos*, meaning "a mass of clouds." A cloud of heavenly hosts has amassed to bear witness to our race, to watch our fight and to record our epic exploits! Just imagine the "who's who" of the faith in the crowd, the celebrities of heaven, the true heroes of God, standing to their feet as the fastest runners in the history of the world grow close to the Celestial Coliseum. Cheering and shouting erupt as we emerge from the dark ages of the shadow of death, grasping tightly our lit torches, holding them high above our heads as we make our way toward the rising of the sun. Our faces are marred with soot; our tunics are soiled with the dirt of those whose souls we rescued from the quagmire of calamity. Our pace increases as we make our way through the tunnel and onto the field, where He awaits us with arms wide open. *"Well done!"* is chanted from the stadium as a wave of raised arms circles through the crowd in honorable adoration.

We are not running for ourselves, but for those who have gone before us—the great cloud of witnesses who are waiting for their reward, which is in us. We are also running this great race for those who are with us, who benefit from our relationship with Jesus. But most profoundly, we are running our race for those who are yet to be born, who will be birthed into our inheritance, who will experience our momentum, and who will stand on our shoulders as we become their great cloud of witnesses!

With all this in mind, it is paramount that we press into the mind of Christ and learn to think like God. The truth is that our level of spiritual intelligence will determine the impact we have on the legacy we leave to future generations. That's right! The more we experience transcended thinking—thinking beyond the confines of time and space, and thinking beyond the limits of human reasoning—the more profound effect we will have on the generations to come. Let's leave the world to come better off than the one we grew up in. May our children's children's children say of us, "That generation truly had the mind of Christ; they were the pioneers of spiritual intelligence who paved the way for our generation."

Spiritual Intelligence Quotient (SQ) Assessment

As you take this SQ assessment, it will reflect the ways that your unique connection to the multifaceted mind of Christ is manifested in your life. It will help you discern your sensitivity to spiritual information, as well as assessing the frequency and relevance of the spiritual information you receive.

Note that this assessment is not intended to anchor you permanently to a certain level or in a specific category of spiritual intelligence. The goal is to launch you into potentially new ways of developing the "spirit of your mind" (see chapter 1).

After you take part 1 of the assessment and tally your results about your SQ level, you will then use your answers to fill in part 2 and gain insight into the primary ways you currently hear from God.

Part 1: Basic Spiritual Intelligence Analysis

In the table that follows, read each of the 25 statements and put the number in the corresponding box that best describes your experience with that statement. For example, if your answer to statement 1 is seldom, put a number 2 in the corresponding **Seldom** column.

If your answer to statement 2 is frequently, put a number 4 in the **Frequently** column. And so on. (For now, disregard the **Category** column of **Think, Know, Feel, See** and **Hear**. We will get to those categories in part 2.)

At the end of these 25 statements, read the analysis of the different score levels to discover some unique things about your SQ level, your potential growth opportunities, and specific action steps you can take to help develop and deepen your spiritual intelligence.

#	Statement	Never = 0	Once = 1	Seldom = 2	Occasionally = 3	Frequently = 4
T H I N K	1 I can identify broken, defective or inefficient systems and then develop sustainable and healthy solutions.					
	2 I have passing or subtle thoughts that end up being accurate.					
	3 I have supernatural wisdom that enables me to understand the process that leads to the truth.					
	4 I receive blueprints, formulas, prototypes or strategies in my mind.					
	5 I mentally process problems and imagine divine solutions.					
K N O W	6 When I don't know what to do, the answer will often just come to me.					
	7 I seem to know details about people that no one has ever told me.					
	8 I hear myself say things that I know I have never heard or learned before.					
	9 I make decisions based on knowledge from an unseen Source.					
	10 I get information or strategies for things I know nothing about.					

#	Statement	Never = 0	Once = 1	Seldom = 2	Occasionally = 3	Frequently = 4
F E E L	11 I have felt someone touch me when no person was visibly present.					
	12 I have a "gut feeling" before something good or bad happens.					
	13 I have physically felt someone else's emotional pain, sickness or physical injury.					
	14 I strongly feel whatever entity is in the spiritual atmosphere.					
	15 I feel and carry the weight of other people's problems or burdens in my body or spirit.					
S E E	16 I have had angelic visitations, and/or I have physically seen demonic manifestations.					
	17 My night dreams come true or provide an accurate source of information.					
	18 I see things like colors, radiance, words or numbers physically appearing on or over people.					
	19 I have open visions that I see with my eyes.					
	20 I readily imagine alternate realities with my mind.					
H E A R	21 I can physically hear people's past experiences, trauma or internal cries of pain.					
	22 I hear the inner Voice of the Spirit instructing, leading or guiding me to positive outcomes.					
	23 I have heard other people's thoughts in my own mind.					
	24 I seem to hear sounds from an unseen source that other people don't hear.					
	25 I have heard the audible voice of God providing helpful instruction or direction.					
	TOTAL for each column:					

Tallying Your Part 1 Score

Step 1   Add up each vertical column's score (under **Never, Once, Seldom, Occasionally** and **Frequently**).

Step 2   Now, add together the scores from all five columns.

TOTAL SCORE: _____

Step 3   Check your total score against the following results to see what part 1 of this test indicates about your level of spiritual intelligence. Remember that your SQ level can change through practice and by taking the recommended action steps to increase your sensitivity and reception.

SQ Total Score 0–25

A score of 0–25 may indicate that you have never had spiritual gifts "AirDropped" to you (see more about spiritual "AirDrops" in chapter 16.) This score may also indicate that you have many gifts, but have relegated your experience to this world's natural laws and to the realms of IQ/EQ only, so are therefore accustomed to "lower" levels of thinking.

Action Step: If this is your SQ score, you have great things ahead as you discover your potential to have the mind of Christ. You can forge new neural pathways and get on the SQ *High*-way of divine wisdom so you can think in new ways (see more about the science behind how we think in chapter 2). Do this by connecting with a community of people who demonstrate spiritual intelligence. This will position you to receive spiritual AirDrops from them that will enable you to have experiences in God that transcend the laws of nature.

SQ Total Score 26–50

A score of 26–50 may indicate that you have an aptitude for spiritual intelligence, but need more experience and/or practice in applying it. Incorporating higher levels of thinking as a way of life, while receiving great feedback from others, will strengthen your connection to the mind of Christ (see chapter 1). It will also build confidence in the gifts God has given you. Stewarding your God-given gifts will enable you to experience different dimensions of spiritual intelligence and supernatural power (see chapter 16's brief overview of several gifts).

Action Step: If this is your SQ score, you have great potential to begin using the gifts you have been given in new ways. When you put your gifts into practice more frequently, it will create space for you to raise your SQ and exercise it on a regular basis. Grow yourself in what you have been given, and gain feedback from those around you who function at a higher level of SQ. Notice the progress you are making, and stay aware of your receptivity to the voice of God.

SQ Total Score 51–75

A score of 51–75 may indicate that you are spiritually intelligent and gain accurate information, but may have skewed results because you lack wisdom on the timing of what you share or with whom you share it (see the "Anachronistic Living" section in chapter 14).

Action Step: If this is your SQ score, God is not only revealing truth to you; He is also imparting the "Spirit of revelation" in you so that you become a co-revealer of truth (see chapter 7). You have much to offer already, but there is still room to grow in applying your SQ to the everyday world you live in. Connect with a mentor who is willing to challenge you with wisdom and authority to help you mature spiritually in the revelatory gifts.

SQ Total Score 76–100

A score of 76–100 may indicate that you are both mature and spiritually intelligent. Your high SQ level is exhibited in your daily relationships and throughout your activities in your community. You are likely motivated by the betterment of mankind, and you demonstrate the powerful gifts you have in a positive and encouraging way. You may identify as one of God's "solutionaries," people who are Christ's answer to the world's problems (see chapter 7).

Action Step: If this is your SQ score, in addition to bringing heaven's solutions to earth's challenges, you can also begin to step into a mentoring or discipling role. Start by equipping those around you who are growing their SQ, especially the next generation, in their giftings and callings. Walk alongside others intentionally and pull out the potential you see in them continually so that they can fulfill the purpose of God in their lives.

Part 2: Basic Receptivity Analysis

Next, look again at the table in part 1 and add up your scores in each category directly following the statement numbers—**Think, Know, Feel, See** and **Hear**. This will help you determine *how* you primarily receive insight and information from God. For example, to get your **Think** score, add together every number in any of the five horizontal rows that begin with the word **Think**. Your score will therefore be between 0 and 20 in each of these categories.

Think = _____

Know = _____

Feel = _____

See = _____

Hear = _____

Using the graph below, shade in your corresponding score in each category so that you can visually compare your spiritual receptivities.

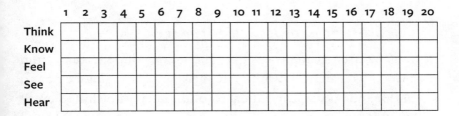

	1	2	3	4	5	6	7	8	9	10	11	12	13	14	15	16	17	18	19	20
Think																				
Know																				
Feel																				
See																				
Hear																				

Jesus lived fully connected with His Father and fully aligned to God's way of thinking. He was what I call "intelligently in tune" with all the extraordinary ways God communicates spiritually with people. I want to focus here on five of the primary ways of spiritual communication that Jesus demonstrated for us, which you just rated yourself on in part 2 of the SQ assessment. These five "receptivity" categories are important indicators of spiritual intelligence, so let's explore each one a little further.

THINK Receptivity

Overview

The SQ receptivity of *thinking* is the ability for someone to process knowledge with divine wisdom. Solomon demonstrated this dynamic when he encountered two harlots arguing over who was the mother of an infant. He did not know the answer, but he supernaturally understood the process of discovering the truth. He wisely decreed that the baby be cut in two so that each woman could have half of the child, which inspired the protective nature of motherhood to come out in the true mother and unearthed the right answer (see 1 Kings 3:16–28).

At the beginning of chapter 13, I shared with you the prophetic word I received that God would give me double wisdom for business.

As we built our companies, the Lord continued to give me divine insights about how to grow our revenue and serve our customers in a way that had never been done in the history of our industry.

Biblical Examples of Jesus the Thinker

Jesus received heavenly insights about everything He did, from choosing His team to His ultimate mission of bringing heaven to earth. He thus became a radical revolutionary who shifted every realm of life. When the world said "an eye for an eye," He declared "love your enemies" (see Matthew 5:38–48). When religious leaders wanted to stone a woman caught in adultery, Jesus asked the person without sin to start the stoning. With that challenge, everyone walked away (see John 8:1–11). He outsmarted His enemies at every turn with wisdom from above, and He left a legacy that still stands as the ultimate pinnacle of supernatural insight.

Are You a Thinker?

The primary way of being intelligently in tune with the mind of Christ as a *thinker* is when the Holy Spirit brings clarity, insight or instruction with supernatural wisdom, giving you the ability to apply knowledge in a way that builds a future envisioned by the Creator. A thinker will receive divine wisdom that will guide him or her to the truth of a matter, and will provide transformative solutions or processes to overcome the problem. This wisdom may be followed by additional "spiritual intel" that comes through supernaturally *knowing*, *feeling*, *seeing* or *hearing* (the other four receptivities).

Thinker Action Step

When facing a complex challenge or circumstance that requires a new perspective, ask the Holy Spirit to give you divine wisdom. Notice any new processes that come to mind or solutions that will advance your problem-solving abilities beyond what is humanly possible.

KNOW Receptivity

Overview

The SQ receptivity of *knowing* makes a person highly perceptive and is predicated by a deep sense of conviction. Spiritual *knowing* is God's way of giving you supernatural information that is not inspired by any natural cause, communication or insight.

I experienced this *knowing* sensitivity when I met a businessman and told him that God was going to give him the secret of magnetic power (see chapter 12). He had not told me that he owned a magnetic invention and innovation company, but I instinctively knew that he carried the keys to magnetic innovation.

Biblical Examples of Jesus the Knower

Jesus demonstrated a value for the spiritual intelligence of *knowing* when He perceived the thoughts, actions and motives of those around Him. For example, He knew when the religious leaders were trying to trap Him (see Matthew 22:15–22). He knew that power had gone out from Him when the woman in the crowd touched His cloak (see Mark 5:21–34). He also knew the intent of the crowd to try to make Him king by force (see John 6:15).

Other biblical examples of this receptivity were when Jesus knew the solution to feeding the multitude, and when He knew where to tell the disciples to cast their nets for a huge catch of fish (see John 6:1–14; Luke 5:1–11). There are also biblical examples of others having this receptivity, for example when Peter knew Ananias and Sapphira were lying about the amount of money they had received for selling some property (see Acts 5:1–11).

Are You a Knower?

The primary way of being intelligently in tune with the mind of Christ as a *knower* occurs when the Holy Spirit brings clarity, insight or instruction about facts, circumstances or situations to your spirit. This may be followed by additional spiritual intel that comes through supernaturally *thinking, feeling, seeing* or *hearing* (the other four receptivities).

Knower Action Step

The gift of *knowing* is an opportunity for others to encounter through you the God of the universe, who understands them intimately and cares for them. Your *knowing* gift will instinctively connect them to the Father of creation, who has numbered the hairs of their head and the days of their life.

It is important for *knowers* to have a high value for information that is instinctive, disconnected from cognitive education or intellectual exploration. Confidence in your gift will grow as the accuracy of your spiritual knowledge is tested. Often, the wisest way to assess the accuracy of your insights is to ask questions of people, rather than make statements about your perceptions (see chapter 4).

FEEL Receptivity

Overview

The SQ receptivity of *feeling* is multisensory, compassionate and highly intuitive. This type of *feeling* leads to a supernatural ability in someone to connect to the internal or external environment of another person, or to sense any demonic or angelic entity that may be affecting the surrounding atmosphere.

You may remember the story in chapter 8 where I got into a car with a friend who was driving and suddenly had this overwhelming feeling that I wanted to kill myself. The feeling I was experiencing actually belonged to my friend, who (unbeknownst to me) was dealing with a spirit of suicide. I prayed for the spirit to leave, and my friend was instantly set free!

Biblical Examples of Jesus the Feeler

Scripture places value on the spiritual intelligence of *feeling* when it describes Jesus as being "touched with the feeling of our infirmities" (see Hebrews 4:15 KJV). Whenever Jesus was moved with compassion in a deep internal sense, He stepped out with solutions of wisdom, healing and power.

Other biblical examples of this receptivity are when Jesus was moved with compassion and healed the blind men's eyes (see Matthew 20:29–34), and when, again filled with compassion, He cleansed a leper (Mark 1:40–45).

Are You a Feeler?

The primary way of being intelligently in tune with the mind of Christ as a *feeler* is when the Holy Spirit brings clarity, insight or instruction through your emotions, or through the ability to feel physically what is present spiritually. A *feeler* will receive divine knowledge through a deep internal (and sometimes emotional) sense, which then may be followed by additional spiritual intel that comes through supernaturally *thinking*, *knowing*, *seeing* or *hearing* (the other four receptivities).

Feeler Action Step

Ask the Holy Spirit to help you become self-aware so that you have insight into your own emotional condition. This will help you differentiate between the intuitive feelings the Holy Spirit gives you and those which are common to your natural humanity.

SEE Receptivity

Overview

The SQ receptivity of *seeing* is visual and imaginative. Ephesians 1:17–21 refers to the spiritual sight as the "eyes of your heart" being opened so that you may "know what is the hope of His calling, what are the riches of the glory of His inheritance in the saints, and what is the surpassing greatness of His power toward us who believe."

I gave a personal example in chapter 3 that exemplifies the receptivity of a seer. In my imagination, I saw a sword in a woman's stomach. That invisible sword signified a condition that was causing intense pain in the woman's abdomen, and when I pulled out the sword, she was instantly healed!

Biblical Examples of Jesus the Seer

Jesus placed value on the spiritual intelligence of *seeing* when He said, "Truly, truly, I say to you, the Son can do nothing of Himself, unless it is something He sees the Father doing" (John 5:19). This example was personified in Jesus when He had a vision of Nathanael under a fig tree (see John 1:43–51).

Other biblical examples of this receptivity are when Isaiah had a vision of the Lord sitting on His throne, Cornelius had a vison of an angel, and John, exiled on the island of Patmos, had a vision of Jesus (see Isaiah 6; Acts 10:1–8; Revelation 1:9–20).

Are You a Seer?

The primary way of being intelligently in tune with the mind of Christ as a *seer* is when the Holy Spirit brings clarity, insight or instruction to you visually. A *seer* will often receive divine knowledge through some form of vision, dream or sanctified imagination, which then may be followed by additional spiritual intel that comes through supernaturally *thinking, knowing, feeling* or *hearing* (the other four receptivities).

Seer Action Step

Ask the Holy Spirit to open the "eyes of your heart." Take notice of your dream life and/or of any new ways that your imagination may engage as God speaks to you. He may give you information such as showing you the angelic realm assigned to your life, or to the lives of other people.

HEAR Receptivity

Overview

The SQ receptivity of *hearing* most likely means that you are highly sensitive to sound, words and the inner voice of the Holy Spirit. This type of *hearing* leads to insight and spiritual understanding outside your natural ability to know things.

I experienced this hearing sensitivity when the Lord gave me specific instructions on how to fix a broken fleet truck that was baffling even the smartest technicians (you can read that story again in chapter 1).

Biblical Examples of Jesus the Hearer

Jesus placed value on the spiritual intelligence of *hearing* when He said, "He who has ears to hear, let him hear" (Matthew 11:15). Other biblical examples include the boy Samuel hearing God's call in the night, Elijah hearing God's instruction in a still, small voice, and Saul the persecutor hearing the voice of God and being converted (see 1 Samuel 3:1–14; 1 Kings 19:9–18; Acts 9:1–19).

Are You a Hearer?

The primary way of being intelligently in tune with the mind of Christ as a *hearer* is when the Holy Spirit speaks through the inner voice and brings clarity, insight or instruction. A *hearer* will typically receive divine knowledge through some form of internal or external sound, which then may be followed by additional spiritual intel that comes through supernaturally *thinking*, *knowing*, *feeling* or *seeing* (the other four receptivities).

Hearer Action Step

Ask the Holy Spirit to give you "ears to hear" His thoughts. Calm your inner world and listen intently for the voice of the Lord in your life. Take time out on a regular basis just to capture the quiet insights of the Holy Spirit.

To investigate the concept of SQ, or spiritual intelligence, further, and to develop your own SQ further, visit sqinstitute.com.

Kris Vallotton is the senior associate leader of Bethel Church in Redding, California, and co-founder of Bethel School of Supernatural Ministry and Bethel Media. He is also the founder of Moral Revolution and Bethel School of Technology, as well as the chairman of Advance Redding. Kris is a bestselling author and has written more than a dozen books and manuals. He is also an international conference speaker and leadership consultant. He and his wife, Kathy, live in Redding and have four children and nine grandchildren. Learn more at krisvallotton.com.

Other Books and Resources by Kris Vallotton

BOOKS

Basic Training for the Prophetic Ministry (workbook)

Destined to Win

Developing a Supernatural Lifestyle

Fashioned to Reign

Heavy Rain

Moral Revolution (with Jason Vallotton)

Outrageous Courage (with Jason Vallotton)

Poverty, Riches and Wealth

School of the Prophets

Spiritual Intelligence

Spirit Wars

The Supernatural Ways of Royalty (with Bill Johnson) and *Basic Training for the Supernatural Ways of Royalty* (workbook)

Winning the War Within (with Jason Vallotton)

RESOURCES

World-Changer Assessment

Poverty, Riches and Wealth E-Course

Spirit Wars E-Course

Destined to Win E-Course

Notable Blog Series

These and many other titles are available at
krisvallotton.com.

Spiritual Intelligence Master Class

*You Have the Mind of Christ
and the Spiritual Capacity for Brilliance*

In the first Master Class of its kind, Kris Vallotton guides you through the reality of what it means to have the mind of Christ. Included with the Master Class is *Basic Training for Spiritual Intelligence*. This manual uses engaging teaching and interactive exercises that will develop your capacity for spiritual intelligence and bring to light God's life-transforming thoughts and ideas. Topically structured with practical applications to enrich your learning, you can create a custom growth plan to expand your spiritual intelligence.

In this journey of discovery, you will

- learn how to build new neural pathways that will increase your spiritual capacity and open you to profound untapped potential
- gain keys to develop the biblical promise of a "renewed mind," including how to access God's thoughts and ideas, so you can bring heaven's solutions to life's challenges
- develop your spiritual aptitude with content that is structured and customized for interactive learning

Launching January 2021!

Visit sqinstitute.com to learn more.

More from Kris Vallotton

In this manual to accompany *Spiritual Intelligence* and his online Master Class, Kris Vallotton guides you through the reality of what it means to have the mind of Christ. The engaging teaching and interactive exercises will help develop your capacity for spiritual intelligence and bring to light God's life-transforming thoughts and ideas.

Basic Training for Spiritual Intelligence by Kris Vallotton
Available January 5, 2021 • sqinstitute.com

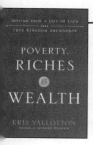

In this eye-opening study of what the Bible really says about money, poverty, riches and wealth, Kris Vallotton will shake up what you thought you knew, showing that Kingdom prosperity always begins from the inside out. When you learn to cultivate a mindset of abundance, you will begin to experience the wealth of heaven in every area of your life.

Poverty, Riches and Wealth by Kris Vallotton • krisvallotton.com

God's crowning creation in the Garden was woman. Yet the state of our world belies her true beauty and purpose. In this compelling book, Kris Vallotton reveals God's true plan and purpose for all women—both in the Church and throughout creation. As sons and daughters of the King, it's time for men and women to work together to restore God's original design for biblical partnership.

Fashioned to Reign by Kris Vallotton • krisvallotton.com

 Chosen

You May Also Like . . .

At this pivotal hour, when evil dominates the headlines and the media persecutes any dissenters, God is searching for men and women who will take a stand in His name. Even now, He is readying a heavy rain of revival. Here is the guidance you need to become a vessel that catches the downpour of the Spirit's rain—and helps release the Kingdom like a flood.

Heavy Rain, revised and updated edition by Kris Vallotton
krisvallotton.com

Amid grueling personal circumstances, Jason Vallotton found himself stunned with grief and a sense of betrayal. Using his story as a poignant illustration of God's grace and healing, Jason invites you to reframe your own understanding of pain in terms of redemption, and discover a restored, fulfilled, and powerful life!

Winning the War Within by Jason Vallotton with Kris Vallotton
jasonvallotton.com

✔Chosen